Ernest Mandel

NLB

The Second Slump

A Marxist Analysis of Recession in the Seventies

Translated by Jon Rothschild

First published as *Ende der Krise oder Krise ohne Ende?*
© Wagenbach Verlag, Berlin, 1977

This revised edition first published 1978
© NLB, 1978
NLB, 7 Carlisle Street, London W1

Phototypeset in Century Schoolbook by
Servis Filmsetting Ltd, Manchester
Printed by Lowe & Brydone Printers Ltd, Thetford, Norfolk, and
bound by Kemp Hall Bindery, Oxford

Designed by Ruth Prentice

ISBN 86091 012 1

Contents

Preface

The analysis in this work attempts to avoid two opposite dangers: a simple recounting of events and the presentation of an analysis so abstract as to be useless in explaining the events that have actually occurred (and will occur). As in my previous works on economic questions, I have attempted at each step to integrate the major features of empirical reality and the analytic categories of Marx, the latter serving to explain the former through a series of mediating analyses, concepts, and hypotheses.

My aim has been to situate the generalized recession of 1974–75 both in its particular historic context – the end of the long period of post-war expansion – and in the more general context of the history of the capitalist mode of production as a whole. I have tried to demonstrate that this recession and the subsequent phase of sluggishness, of hesitant, uneven, and noncumulative recovery, are the products neither of chance nor of extraneous factors (such as the rises in oil prices, the 'liberation struggle of the peoples of the third world', the 'irrational behaviour of the trade unions', 'excessive wage demands by the workers', and so on). On the contrary, the recession and the subsequent depressive recovery correspond to the inherent logic of the system, although extraneous or accidental factors obviously do play a role in determining the particular features of each cycle.

Along the way, I shall be able to refine the exposition and application of the Marxist theory of periodic crises and of the industrial cycle, which remains one of the most controversial –

and most impressive – chapters of the theoretical work of Karl Marx.

It is scarcely necessary to emphasize that although the author has striven for maximum *objectivity* – to grasp and explain reality as it exists in its shifting totality, disregarding no aspect in an effort to tailor the real world to this or that pre-conceived ideological schema – he is not at all *impartial*.

The crisis, the reappearance of massive unemployment, the universal offensive of capital against the rights of the working class, the mounting threats to democratic rights and peace as a very function of the deterioration of the economic situation of capital – all these things move me to re-emphasize that the capitalist system is doomed.

Increasingly, it is threatening to destroy the very substance of the material civilization and culture whose rise it previously assured, albeit in a contradictory manner, with the enormous defects and instances of alienation that were always inherent in this system. It is urgent to replace it with a social system that conforms to the needs of humanity, to its contemporary potential, its productive forces, and its yearning for emancipation: the socialist system. The only force capable of completing such a gigantic task of reconstruction is the working class, all the wage -earners.

The present crisis should make it easier to extract the working class from the grip of bourgeois ideology, for it is tearing off the veils that had partially concealed the real face of capitalism during the period of relative prosperity. The crisis thus favours a rise in proletarian class consciousness, which will stimulate the anti-capitalist struggle. But if the weapon of class consciousness is to be rigorously scientific, it must entail neither lie nor legend nor myth but must be based on the real facts and their explanation. Such is our ambition. Such should be the ambition of all Marxists, for whom only the truth can be revolutionary.

1

A Crisis of
Over-Production

In 1974 and 1975 the international capitalist economy suffered its first generalized recession since the end of the Second World War. It was the first recession that struck *all* the great imperialist powers simultaneously. Although it surprised all those in bourgeois and petty-bourgeois circles, and even in the workers' movement, who had given credence to claims that the governments of capital are now able to 'control the cycle',[1] revolutionary Marxists had foreseen the crisis and predicted its outbreak, almost to the exact date.[2]

The generalized recession was the most serious of the post-

[1] Innumerable sources could be cited. For example, Paul Samuelson, winner of the Nobel Prize for Economics: 'The National Bureau of Economic Research has worked itself out of one of its first jobs, namely business cycles' (National Bureau of Economic Research Colloquium on 'The Business Cycle Today', 24 September 1970). Samuelson again, this time in his *Economics*, hundreds of thousands of copies of which have been sold: 'Neo-classical synthesis: by means of appropriately reinforcing monetary and fiscal policies, our mixed-enterprise system can avoid the excesses of boom and slump and can look forward to healthy progressive growth' (New York, fourth edition, 1958, p. 360). See also Walter Heller, *New Dimensions of Political Economy*, New York 1967, p. 104, and Sir Roy Harrod, *Money*, London 1969, pp. 188, 190. As for authors associated with the workers' movement, let us recall the theses of John Strachey in *Contemporary Capitalism*, Baran and Sweezy in *Monopoly Capital*, and Castoriades, all of whom emphasized the allegedly proven effectiveness of anti-cyclical techniques, or of the policies of the monopolies, or of a combination of both, in 'regularizing' the market of the capitalist economy and averting serious crises.

[2] Cf. the theses on the 'New Rise of World Revolution' adopted by the Ninth World Congress of the Fourth International in April 1969, in *Intercontinental Press*, vol. 7, no. 26, July 14, 1969, p. 673, and the general political resolution adopted by the Tenth World Congress in February 1974, in *Intercontinental Press*, vol. 12, no. 46, December 23, 1974, p. 1722.

war period precisely because it was generalized. The lack of synchronization of the industrial cycle during the period 1948–68 had reduced the scope of recessions. A decline in production and domestic demand in the countries hit by a recession (for example, the United States in 1960 or West Germany in 1966–67) had previously been compensated by an expansion of exports to countries that had escaped the crisis. This time, however, the international synchronization of the conjunctural shifts in the major imperialist countries intensified the downward trend in economic activity.

A good example of this may be seen in the evolution of the cycle in West Germany. The recession began during the second quarter of 1974, which was the first quarter marked by an absolute decline in the gross national product, to the order of 0.5%. But it must be emphasized that GNP had risen by only 1% during the first quarter of 1974, while exports were still rising 9.5%. It is thus evident that the continued strong expansion of exports retarded the outbreak of the recession in West Germany by at least a quarter.

During two successive quarters, the second and third of 1974, West German exports ceased to rise. Neither did they decline, however; they simply stagnated. Since GNP diminished by 0.5% during each of these quarters, it seems that the maintenance of West German exports at their maximum level curbed the recession and confined it during the second and third quarters of 1974.

During the fourth quarter of 1974 and the first quarter of 1975, however, West German exports declined 3.5% and 8.5% respectively, under the impact of the international recession. Suddenly, the recession intensified in West Germany. GNP fell by 2% and 1.5% respectively during these two quarters. The increasingly profound integration of the West German economy into the international economy had enabled the 1966–67 recession to be limited. Some people thought that this would also be the case in 1974. Helmut Schmidt, for example, imprudently stated at the September 1974 congress of the metalworkers' union: 'The degree to which our economy is doing well in comparison with the international economy is almost embarrassing.' By the end of 1974 Schmidt would have to eat those words. This time West Germany's growing integration into the international economy was to aggravate the crisis rather than alleviate it.[3]

This synchronization of the international industrial cycle is not at all fortuitous. It results from profound economic transformations which occurred during the preceding long period of expansion. It is, in a certain sense, the ineluctable result of that expansion.

The post-war boom had given powerful impetus to a new rise in the productive forces, to a new technological revolution. The result was a new leap forward in the concentration of capital and the internationalization of production, the productive forces increasingly overstepping the limits of the bourgeois national state. (This tendency began to emerge back at the beginning of the century, but it intensified considerably after 1948.) The international division of labour among the imperialist countries as a whole progressed strongly. From the standpoint of the organization of capital – of what Marx called 'functioning capital' – this was reflected in the rise of multinational corporations each of which produces surplus-value in several different countries simultaneously. At the dawn of the imperialist era such firms operated essentially in the raw materials sector. Today their sphere of activity is spreading to nearly all sectors of transformation industry properly so called.

This internationalization of production, which under the capitalist system inevitably takes the form of ever more advanced international concentration and centralization of capital, runs increasingly counter to the attempts of the 'national' imperialist states successfully to apply anti-cyclical policies, the impact of which remains essentially limited to national frontiers.[4]

[3] For the specific analysis concerning West Germany in this work, see Winfried Wolf, 'Westdeutsche Wirtschaftskrise 1974/75 und Aufschwung 1976/77', pp. 141–2, in Ernest Mandel and Winfried Wolf, *Ende der Krise oder Krise ohne Ende?*, Berlin, 1977.

[4] '... in the domain of international relations, it clearly seems that the multinational corporation can rather easily carry the day against states which have never been able to federate. Thus, the great important decisions on re-

The principal technique through which bourgeois governments have sought to 'control' the economic cycle since 1945
has been the policy of successive expansion and contraction of
credit, in other words, of bank money and the money supply as
a whole (of 'total demand'). The principal technique for curbing
the scope of periodic over-production crises during the past
twenty-five years, then, has been to expand credit and the
money supply. (This amounts, of course, to efforts to *reduce the
scope* of the crises and not to prevent their outbreak; in this the
bourgeoisie is as incapable as ever.) Thus, from the standpoint
of the functioning of the international capitalist economy as a
whole, the major characteristic of the long phase of post-war
expansion was the emergence of *credit cycles partially independent* of the industrial cycle, the former attempting to
'compensate for' the latter. But since capitalist states, central
banks, and currencies remain national, these credit cycles were
also 'national', and rather de-synchronized internationally.
Each imperialist government was able to apply 'its' credit
policy 'flexibly', depending on the fluctuations of the world
market as reflected in fluctuations in national balances of
payments.

But anti-crisis techniques were and remain thoroughly inflationary. In the long run, repeated application of a policy of
monetary expansion every five or six years inevitably leads to a
universal acceleration of inflation. When inflation accelerated
in *all* the imperialist countries and led to the collapse of the
international monetary system, symbolized by the proclamation that the dollar was no longer convertible for gold, all the
imperialist governments were compelled to apply anti-inflation
policies simultaneously, even if only under the pressure of
competition. This gave a new impetus to the international
synchronization of the industrial cycle.

Finally, precisely because the long phase of post-war expansion was drawing to a close, because the principal motor forces

deployment should more and more frequently be those of the great enterprises
of worldwide inclination, shifting among states in accordance with events,
sites, and epochs' (Professor A. Cotta, in *Synthèses*, no. 14, fourth quarter,
1976).

of the expansion were beginning to wear down, and because the long-term expansion of production had inevitably to slow down, the contradictions of the capitalist economy asserted themselves more strongly, within each imperialist country, among these countries as a whole, and between them and the semi-colonial and dependent countries. The 'boom' phases were condemned to be of shorter duration (that of 1972–73 was to a large extent speculative). The phases of stagnation, and even recession, would be longer. This obviously facilitates the international synchronization of the cycle. Recessions that last only six months spread from country to country less easily than those that last two years.

The generalized recession is thus a synthetic expression of the reversal of the 'long wave of expansion' (which began in the United States in 1940, in West Europe and Japan in 1948, and lasted until the end of the sixties). I had predicted this reversal as early as 1964, and my *Late Capitalism* is largely devoted to it.[5]

The new 'long wave' was to be characterized by a medium- to long-term growth rate probably 50% inferior to that of the fifties and sixties. The expansive fever of those two decades would be long in returning. Even more important, however, has been the emergence of another factor, symbolized by May 1968 in France, the 'creeping May' in Italy, the Portuguese revolutionary process of 1974–75, and the spectacular upsurge of workers' struggles in Britain and Spain, phenomena that will also spread, sooner or later, to West Germany, the United States, and Japan: the general social crisis of bourgeois society, a crisis of capitalist relations of production, and of all bourgeois social relations. This crisis has become intertwined with the lasting slowdown in capitalist economic growth, thus accentuating and aggravating the effects of conjunctural economic fluctuations and in turn receiving fresh stimulus from these fluctuations.

[5] 'L'Apogée du néo-capitalisme et ses lendemains' in *Temps Modernes*, no. 219–220 (August–September 1964); *Late Capitalism*, NLB, London, 1975. An interesting recent work devoted to the same subject is H. Jacot, *Croissance économique et fluctuations conjoncturelles*, Lyon, 1976.

1. The Scope of the 1974-75 Recession

In 1975 industrial production and gross national product were on the decline in *all* the major imperialist countries compared with the preceding year. Table 1 presents the extent of the decline in industrial production between the 'peak' of the boom and the lowest point of the recession:

Table 1

Difference Between Maximum Industrial Production Before the Recession and Minimum Industrial Production During the Recession in the Major Imperialist Countries

Country	Quarter of Maximum Production	Quarter of Minimum Production	Fall in Production
United States	4th 1973	2nd 1975	14.4%
Canada	1st 1974	3rd 1975	6.9%
Japan	4th 1973	1st 1975	19.8%
West Germany	4th 1973	3rd 1975	11.8%
France	3rd 1974	3rd 1975	13.6%
Britain	4th 1973	4th 1974	10.1%
Italy	2nd 1974	3rd 1975	15.5%
Netherlands	1st 1974	3rd 1975	11.7%
Belgium	1st 1974	3rd 1975	17.1%
Sweden	3rd 1974	2nd 1975	4.1%
Switzerland	2nd 1974	1st 1975	20.3%
Spain	April 1974	April 1975	10.0%

Source: OECD, *Perspectives Economiques*, no. 19, July 1976, p. 47; for Spain: Spanish statistics.

It is striking to note the discrepancy between the reduction in industrial production, much more modest than during the great economic crisis of 1929-32, and the quite considerable level of unemployment provoked by the 1974-75 recession. On the average – with a few, sometimes important differences from country to country, West Germany being the big exception – unemployment attained fully half the level of the great crisis. Even during the 1969-71 recession there were 10 million unemployed in the imperialist countries taken as a whole. During the winter of 1975-76, when unemployment peaked, the total number of officially recognized unemployed in all the imperial-

ist countries was close to 17 million. Table 2 shows the breakdown by country.

Table 2

Maximum Unemployment During the 1974–75 Recession

Country	Quarter and year	Number unemployed
United States	4th 1975	7,912,000
Britain	3rd 1976	1,319,000
Japan	4th 1975	1,178,000
Italy	3rd 1976	1,145,000
West Germany	4th 1975	1,141,000
France	3rd 1976	1,036,000
Spain	4th 1976	800,000
Canada	4th 1975	724,000
Australia	4th 1975	297,000
Belgium	3rd 1976	292,000
Netherlands	4th 1975	211,000
Denmark	4th 1975	111,000
Other imperialist countries	4th 1975	600,000

Sources: For the fourth quarter of 1975: United Nations, *Supplément à l'étude
sur l'économie mondiale 1975*; for the third quarter of 1976: *Financial Times*,
25 October 1976, *Eurostat* (EEC); for Spain: Spanish statistics.

The fact that unemployment was much more pronounced
than the decline in production is essentially accounted for by
two factors:

(1) Industrial activity in the imperialist countries still bears
the stamp of the third technological revolution, the introduction of semi-automatic and automatic production techniques.
The result is a rapid augmentation of the physical productivity
of labour, especially in capitalist Europe and Japan. (In the
United States the same phenomenon had already occurred
during a previous phase. The sources of the augmentation of
productivity have even begun to wear down in the United
States, except in a few industrial branches, like steel, automobiles, and shipbuilding, whose productivity is markedly
inferior to the most advanced productivity rates in West
Europe and Japan.) Now, if productivity rises 5% a year, a
similar rise in production is required if the volume of productive employment is to be maintained, other things being equal.
If the work force is growing 1% a year, a 6% increase in pro-

duction would be required to maintain the volume of productive employment. A 2% decline in production accompanied by a 4% increase in physical productivity and a 0.5% increase in the work force will provoke an increase in unemployment of approximately 6%.

(2) In order to reconstruct the industrial reserve army of labour during the long post-war expansion, capital had incorporated a great number of married women, youth, and immigrant workers from less industrialized countries into the mass of actual or potential wage earners. These categories were in general poorly paid, restricted to unskilled and/or unhealthy spheres of activity, and employed only marginally. They were thus vulnerable to easy and massive expulsion from the process of production as soon as a fundamental reversal of the industrial cycle occurred. It is therefore not at all astonishing that such an expulsion did indeed take place on a grand scale during the 1974–75 recession. The unemployment rate is consequently much higher among these three sectors of the proletariat than among male, adult, indigenous white- and blue-collar workers.

The effects of the 1974–75 recession were undoubtedly aggravated by the fact that at the beginning of the recession inflation was not only not reabsorbed under the effects of over-population, but even accelerated in many countries. The inflation rates in the major imperialist countries are indicated in Table 3.

Table 3

Rate of Increase in Cost of Living in Major Imperialist Countries

Country	1973	1974	First half of 1975 (annual rate)
United States	6.2%	11.0%	12.8%
West Germany	6.9%	7.0%	6.0%
Japan	19.1%	21.9%	14.1%
France	7.3%	13.7%	9.5%
Britain	9.1%	16.1%	23.5%
Italy	10.8%	21.9%	14.1%
Belgium	7.0%	12.7%	15.3%

Source: OECD.

Indeed, when a sharp increase in the cost of living coincides with a sudden upsurge of massive unemployment, the consequent reduction in purchasing power is more than proportional to the reduction in employment – unless, which has hardly ever been the case, unemployment compensation rises faster than the cost of living. In addition, the persistence or even accentuation of a high rate of inflation increases pressure on all governments to apply a deflationary policy, at the very moment that an anti-crisis policy would require an expansion of credit and the money supply. During the 1974–75 recession pressure in this direction, for the first time since 1929–32, was so strong that no government in any major imperialist country dared apply anti-cyclical measures on a grand scale from the beginning of the recession. Only a few, smaller imperialist countries commanding exceptional reserves or room for manoeuvre – especially Sweden, Austria, and for a time Norway – continued to commit themselves in this direction, Austria and Norway with notable success, Sweden succeeding only in retarding, but not preventing, a pronounced contraction of productive activity.

If the cost of living rises sharply despite the existence of significant inventories of unsold commodities and significant excess production capacity in the factories of the consumer goods sector, this is fundamentally a result of price control by the great monopolies in this sector. These monopolies are able to eliminate price competition to some extent, and even to increase prices in the event of a decline in their rate of utilization of productive capacity, the aim being to compensate for the increase in fixed cost per unit caused by the sales slump and the under-utilization of existing capacity. They thus succeed in maintaining profit margins and in averting an excessively catastrophic fall in the rate of profit.[6] But they can implement this scheme only with the complicity of governments, central

---

[6] In this regard see the interesting study of Rudolf Hickel, 'Oekonomische Stabilisierungspolitik in der Krise', Bremen, 1976, which takes up and expands the reference to American sources which we had already used in this regard in *Late Capitalism*. On the limits of this price policy of the monopolies, see Chapter 5.

banks, and the banking system as a whole; despite all the sermons about the 'priority of the struggle against inflation', these agencies continue to inflate the money supply in accordance with the needs of the monopolies.

Under free-competition capitalism – or under a pure gold standard system – such techniques would obviously be impossible. (Indeed, even now, under the rule of the monopolies, they are possible only to a certain, not unlimited extent; in the long run the law of value eventually holds sway. We will return to this important aspect of the problem further on.) But this does not mean that the over-production crisis is necessarily less profound or of shorter duration when resulting from a general collapse of prices. The crises of 1920–21 and 1929–32, both of which were marked by heavy price declines, demonstrate the contrary. The rate of unemployment was even higher during the 'golden age' of capitalism than it is today.[7] We may add that a lack of synchronization of the industrial cycle and the cycle of agricultural surpluses accentuated inflation in 1973 and 1974, years characterized by a pronounced fall in world grain reserves and therefore by pronounced increases in the prices of food products. We shall return to this point below pp. 140–41ff.

The apologists for the system can deny the gravity of the crisis racking the international capitalist economy only by systematically underestimating the scope of the recession and by concealing the facts. This is particularly the case for a team of neo-liberal economists directed by Professors Emil Claasen and Pascal Salin, among which we find such leading lights as Nobel Prize winner Milton Friedman and Professor J. Rueff. They go so far as to write: 'In general, a great depression can be defined by two elements. On the one hand, gross national product must diminish by 3% to 5%, and over a period of several

[7] See the interesting article by Richard B. du Boff, 'Unemployment in the United States, A Historical Summary' in *Monthly Review*, vol. 29, no. 6 (November 1977). Du Boff gives the following pre-1915 rates of unemployment (as a percentage of the civilian work force): 1890: 4%; 1891: 5.4%; 1892: 3%; 1893: 11.7%; 1894: 18.4%(!); 1895: 13.7%; 1896: 14.4%; 1897: 14.5%; 1898: 12.4%; 1899: 6.5%; 1900: 5.0%; 1901: 4%; 1902: 3.7%; 1903: 3.9%; 1904: 5.4%; 1905: 4.3%; 1906: 1.7%; 1907: 2.8%; 1908: 8%; 1909: 5.1%; 1910: 5.9%; 1911: 6.7%; 1912: 4.6%; 1913: 4.3%; 1914: 7.9%.

years; in the United States in 1974–75 there was only a recession, that is, a decline in the gross national product during at least two quarters.[8] And they strongly insist on the allegation that there was no contraction of world trade (of exports) in 1974–75.

2. Contraction in World Trade

For twenty years the exports of the capitalist countries had risen more rapidly than their industrial production. This trend was particularly noticeable in the imperialist countries themselves. Between 1953 and 1963 the volume of industrial production in the capitalist countries rose 62%, while exports rose 82%. Between 1963 and 1972 industrial production rose 65%, exports 111%. But in 1975, for the first time since the beginning of the long phase of post-war economic expansion, the volume of exports diminished. The Organization of Economic Co-operation and Development (OECD) evaluates this decline at 7% for world trade as a whole (including trade involving the non-capitalist countries), and this suggests an even greater rate of contraction for the international trade of the capitalist countries alone, since exchanges between non-capitalist countries continued to grow.

Granted, the contraction of world trade did not coincide with the beginning of the generalized recession. But it became inevitable once this recession had spread to all the imperialist countries, since they still constitute the predominant sector of the world market (of 'worldwide available purchasing power'). As early as the first half of 1975 the *value* of the exports of several capitalist countries was on the decline (the *volume* of exports was on the decline everywhere, taking account of the persistent price increases). During the second half of 1975 the fall in the value of exports spread to the majority of the great imperialist countries, only the United States and Italy escaping the general trend (the case of American exports is distorted by

[8] *Turbulences d'une économie prospère*, collection edited by Emile Claasen and Pascal Salin, Paris, 1978, p. 20.

the significant weight of this country's food exports. If manufacturing products alone are counted, U.S. exports were also on the decline as of the second half of 1975.) The figures are in Table 4.

Table 4

Exports by Half-year, in thousands of millions of current dollars

Country	2nd Half-year 1974	1st Half-year 1975	2nd Half-year 1975
United States	51.6	52.9	55.2
West Germany	47.2	47.6	45.2
Japan	29.5	28.3	26.8
France	24.7	26.8	25.9
Britain	19.7	21.2	20.3
Canada	17.8	16.5	17.0
Italy	16.5	16.7	17.0

Source: OECD, *Economic Outlook*, no. 18, December 1975.

The contraction of the volume of world trade resulted fundamentally from the interaction of three factors:

(1) It was the direct product of the recession in the imperialist countries, in that the fall of production and employment reduced overall demand for imported consumer goods and capital goods (including, incidentally, overall demand for raw materials).

(2) It was the indirect product of the recession in that the exporting countries (especially those exporting raw materials, except oil) suffered a sharp reduction in their currency resources following the decline in the volume and price of their exports; they were thus compelled to reduce their imports.

(3) It was the product of the deliberate policy of import reductions applied particularly by certain imperialist powers that suffered heavy balance of payments deficits during the first half of 1974; in other words, it was the product of a scarcely disguised return to economic nationalism and protectionism.

This latter policy, it may be noted, was largely successful in some cases. Japan, whose trade balance for the period March 1973 to March 1974 showed a deficit of $13.5 thousand million, was able to absorb this deficit completely by the second quarter of 1975. For the period March 1974 to March 1975 Japan's trade balance even showed a surplus of $4 thousand million. There was a similar reversal in the United States, whose trade deficit for the third quarter of 1974 stood at an annual equivalent of $8 thousand million and was turned into a surplus of $1.3 thousand million for the first quarter of 1975. Italy succeeded in reducing its trade deficit by 75%. Even in Britain the situation was very clearly redressed, the trade balance improving by $7 thousand million between autumn 1974 and spring 1975. Finally, for France the March 1974 trade deficit of 2 thousand million francs became a surplus of 620 million francs in March 1975.

These successes were achieved with the aid of all sorts of import restrictions, as well as modifications in exchange rates conceived so as to favour exports at the expense of imports. (The most pronounced case was that of the pound sterling, which was 'floated' so as to lose 25% of its value relative to the realignment of currencies in December 1971.) Obviously, there had to be losers in this 'zero sum game'. They were essentially some minor imperialist countries (among them Spain, Switzerland, Denmark, and Portugal) and the semi-colonial countries – including, incidentally, the oil exporters.

The balance of trade between the oil exporters and the imperialist countries shifted sharply in the course of the recession. The trade surplus of the oil exporting countries was initially evaluated at more than $80 thousand million for 1974, but this figure had to be successively revised downward. In the end, it came to about $60 thousand million. Moreover, it continued to shrink throughout 1975, under the twofold effects of the world decline in oil sales (resulting from both the price increases and the recession) and the spectacular increase in the volume and costs of the imports of the oil exporting countries. This increase was already of the order of 75% in the first quarter of 1975 compared with the first quarter of 1974; and in 1974 it had been 70% higher than in 1973. Further on we shall return to the implications of this turnabout in the balance of payments trend.

3. A Classic Over-Production Crisis

The generalized recession of 1974–75 was a classic over-production crisis. This must be asserted all the more categorically since many sources have sought, in the interests of a cause that is not purely ideological, to assign responsibility for the generalized recession to the 'oil sheikhs' or the trade unions and their 'excessive wage increases'. The classic character of the 1974–75 recession becomes striking when one considers two features which dominate the more long-term evolution of the economic cycle.

The 1974–75 recession was the outcome of a typical phase of decline of the rate of profit. This decline clearly *predated* the pronounced rise in oil prices that followed the October War of 1973. The figures in Table 5 indicate this.

Table 5

Rate of Profit (after Elimination of Gains of Reappreciation of Inventories) on Capital of Non-financial Companies in the United States

Year	Before taxes	After taxes
1948–50	16.2%	8.6%
1951–55	14.3%	6.4%
1956–60	12.2%	6.2%
1961–65	14.1%	8.3%
1966–70	12.9%	7.7%
1970	9.1%	5.3%
1971	9.6%	5.7%
1972	9.9%	5.6%
1973	10.5%	5.4%

Source: William D. Nordhaus, 'The Falling Share of Profit', in A. M. Okun and L. Perry (eds.), *Brookings Papers on Economic Activity*, No. 1, 1974, the Brookings Institution, Washington DC, p. 180.

Gross profits (before taxes) of all American corporations continued to decline, from an annual level of $155 thousand million for the third quarter of 1974 to $135 thousand million for the fourth quarter of 1974 and $100 thousand million for the first quarter of 1975. The decline in net profits was 25% over the same period. According to the statistics of *Conference Board*, the profit margins of non-financial American corporations dropped from an average of 20–22% for the period 1959–66 to 12% during the recession of 1970–71; they climbed back to 15% during the 'speculative boom' of 1972–73 and fell again to 11–12% at the beginning of 1975.

In West Germany experts estimate that the decline in the gross incomes of companies (less fictitious 'entrepreneurial salaries' and compared with the net assets of these companies) was about 20% between 1960 and 1968 (the year of the economic upturn, with a sharp new rise in profits after the recession of 1966–67); there was a further decline of 25% between 1968 and 1973. Three years later, the same expert report published a graph showing the share of gross income of company profits and capital as a percentage of the value of production. It declined from 10% in 1960 to 8% in 1966, 9% in 1968, 6% in 1972, 4.5% in 1975, and 5% in 1977.[9]

The evolution of the rate of profit in Britain has been evaluated as shown in Table 6.

Table 6

Rate of Profit (after Deduction of Gains of Reappreciation of Inventories) on Net Holdings of Industrial and Commercial Companies in Britain

Year	Before taxes	After taxes
1950–54	16.5%	6.7%
1955–59	14.7%	7.0%
1960–64	13.0%	7.0%
1965–69	11.7%	5.3%
1968	11.6%	5.2%
1969	11.1%	4.7%
1970	9.7%	4.1%

Source: Andrew Glyn and Bob Sutcliffe, *British Capitalism, Workers and the Profits Squeeze*, London, 1971, p. 66.

The Economist formulated the classic phrase concerning British industry's hesitation to 'step up' productive investment: profits first, investments later.' According to its calculations, the index of company profits fell from 100 in 1964 to less

[9] *Sachverständigenrate zur Begutachtung der Gesamtwirtschaftlichen Entwicklung*, Jahresgutachten, 1974; ibid, Jahresgutachten, 1977–78, p. 57.

than 60 in 1975, with a particularly rapid decline between 1973 and 1975 (from an index of 90 to one less than 60).[10]

In Japan there was a decline of 35.5% in the gross profits and 20.9% in the net profits of the country's 174 largest companies during the fiscal year 1974–75, which ended on 31 March 1975. Profits fell 56% in the manufacturing industries, only 19.3% in the other sectors. This fall in the average rate of profit in Japan, moreover, is part of a more long-term trend, as may be seen in Table 7.

Table 7

Rate of Profit (after Deduction of Gains of Reappreciation of Inventories) on Gross Holdings of Industrial, Commercial, and Financial Companies in Japan

Year	Before taxes
1963	12.5%
1964	12.8%
1965	11.9%
1966	12.4%
1967	14.0%
1968	14.7%
1969	14.3%
1970	14.7%
1971	14.2%
1972	13.0%
1973	10.9%
1974	11.9%

Source: OECD, McCracken Report, Paris, June 1977, p. 366.

According to the McCracken report, the average gross profit rate in Italy declined at an average annual rate of 5.6% during the period 1966–69. The fall was 4.9% in 1970; 4.3% in 1971; 4.2% in 1972; 4% in 1973; 3.3% in 1974; and 3% in 1975.

Graph I depicts the trajectory of the rate of profit in Sweden. The major Swedish bank commected: 'The profit erosion, dangerous in the long run, which has gradually appeared in far too many cases in the last ten years, is the price paid for being able to maintain high exports.'[11]

[10] *The Economist*, 6 September 1975.
[11] Skandinavska Enskilda Banken, *Quarterly Review*, nos. 1–2, 1977.

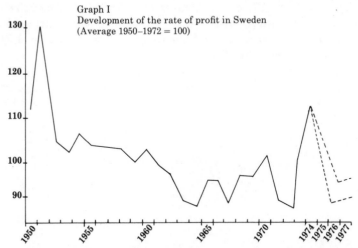

Graph I
Development of the rate of profit in Sweden
(Average 1950–1972 = 100)

Gross figures have been calculated on a percentage basis in relation to turn-over, as profits before deduction of depreciation, interest payments and taxes.

Source for 1950–1974, *Neue Zurcher Zeitung*, 8–9th May 1976; for 1975–1977, figures from the Swedish Industrial Federation.

As for France, Professor Christian Goux calculates a fall in profit rates from 18.2% in 1970 to 11.1% in 1976.[12] The proportion of profit to value-added in non-agricultural enterprises evolved in the following manner: 1971: 40.1%; 1972: 39.9%; 1973: 38.5%; 1974: 37.3%; 1975: 36.1%.[13]

[12] *Ruptures d'un système économique*, edited by Xavier Greffe and Jean-Louis Reiffers, Paris, 1978, p. 286.

[13] The relationship of profits to value-added is closer to the rate of surplus-value than to the rate of profit. The McCracken report suggests that there was no decline in the rate of profit in France in the years preceding the crisis. Nevertheless, an INSEE study entitled 'Fresque historique du système productif' (October 1974) confirms the deterioration of the relation of fixed capital to product beginning in 1964; Jacques Mairesse had already called attention to this in a study which appeared in *Economie et Statistiques* (July–August 1971). From this deterioration one can derive the indices of a falling trend in the rate of profit expressed in the categories of Marxist theory, by incorporating the evolution of the cost of raw materials (constant capital is, in fact, the sum of fixed capital and circulating constant capital, that is, the value of the raw materials transformed in the process of production) and by deducting from 'product' the wage bill of the productive workers and the amortization of fixed capital (INSEE, *Comptes de la nation 1976*, Paris, 1977).

The fact that the deeper causes of the 1974–75 generalized recession predate the rise in oil prices is also demonstrated by the regular increase in *excess capacity in industry* as revealed in American statistics (Table 8).

Table 8

Rate of Utilization of Productive Capacity in Manufacturing Industry in the United States

1966: 92% (boom)
1967: 78% (mini-recession)
1968: 87.7% (boom)
1969: 86.5% (boom)
1970: 78% (recession)
1971: 75% (recession)
1972: 78.5% (boom)
1973: 83% (boom)
1974: 78% (recession)
March 1975: 65% (recession)
June 1975: 68.5% (recession)
December 1975: 73.5% (recovery)

Source: Statistics published monthly by *Business Week*.

This long-term deterioration – in each boom and each recession the rate of utilization of the productive apparatus declines in comparison with the corresponding phase of the preceding cycle – becomes especially pronounced when account is taken of the enormous amount of American production wasted on military or paramilitary products. If we take this factor into consideration, we arrive at a *virtually permanent non-utilization of nearly one-third of existing productive capacity in the United States.* There could be no better demonstration of the present crisis as a classic capitalist overproduction crisis.

The reversal of the 'long wave of expansion' lasting from the forties to the end of the sixties is equally classic. The long accelerated post-war expansion resulted from the super-exploitation of the working class effected by fascism and the Second World War (and in the United States by the cold war, with its disastrous effects on the workers' movement). This permitted a pronounced rise in the rate of surplus-value and hence in the rate of profit, which in turn permitted the heightened accumulation of capital that set the third technological revolution in motion on a grand scale (semi-automation, nuclear energy, etc.). By considerably increasing the production of relative surplus-value and the super-profits of the most technologically advanced monopolies ('technological profits'), this development permitted prolongation of the expansion under conditions that were 'ideal' for capital: *both* a heightened rate of profit *and* a rising real standard of living for the toiling masses, that is, an expanding market.

But the third technological revolution, like the expansion itself, implied an accentuated concentration of capital, which led to a pronounced increase in the organic composition of capital. The long period of full employment considerably strengthened the objective weight of the working class, the power of its mass organizations (above all the trade unions), and its combativity, in accordance with an autonomous cycle of class struggle on an international scale. Thus, from the 1960s capital faced mounting difficulties in compensating for the rise in the organic composition of capital with a continuous rise in the rate of surplus-value. Hence the inexorable crumbling of the average rate of profit, which, in correlation with the increasingly universal spread of the features of the third technological revolution (and therefore the erosion of 'technological profits'), wound up causing the reversal of the 'long wave'.

Many authors have failed to grasp this imbrication of the 'oil crisis' and the more long-term reversal of the economic trend signalled by the extension of excess capacity (i.e. mounting over-production) on the one hand and the fall in the average rate of profit on the other hand. For instance, in 1974 Edmond Alphandéry and Georges Delsupéhé were still centring their analysis exclusively on the manipulation of aggregate demand by governments. They thus envisaged continuous growth: 'The trend shaping up is thus one of progressive recovery, with lower inflation rates and a relaxation of short-term interest rates, because of the decline in inventories.'[14] We know what actually happened.

[14] *Les Politiques de stabilisation*, Paris, 1974, pp. 161, 180.

Every over-production crisis in the history of capitalism has combined general features related to the fundamental contradictions of the capitalist mode of production with particular features resulting from the precise historical moment of the development of that mode of production in which it occurs. The generalized recession of 1974–75 was no exception to this rule.

Two particular features of this recession ought to be stressed. First, there was a progressive shift, brought about by the inevitable acceleration of inflation and the anticipatory responses this provoked,[15] from inflation as a stimulant of economic activity to the *stagflation* of 1970–71 and then the *slumpflation* of 1974–75. Inflation gradually ceased to have a stimulating effect on capitalist productive activity as a whole and even began to have perverse effects. At the same time, larger and larger doses of inflation were needed to stimulate 'aggregate demand'. The figures on the acceleration of inflation, shown in Table 9, are unequivocal. (And it should be noted that the rise in oil prices can account for an inflation rate of no more than 2% for all the imperialist countries.)

Table 9

Annual Rate of Increase of Consumer Prices (according to official statistics) in %

Country	Average 1960–65	1968	1969	1970	1971	1972	1973	1974	1975
United States	1.3	4.2	5.4	5.9	4.3	3.3	6.2	11.0	7.8
Japan	6.2	5.5	5.2	7.6	6.3	4.3	11.7	21.0	11.9
Britain	3.6	4.8	5.4	6.4	9.5	7.0	9.2	16.1	22.1
West Germany	2.8	1.6	1.9	3.4	5.3	5.5	6.9	7.0	6.1
France	3.8	4.8	6.4	5.3	5.5	5.9	7.3	13.7	11.7
Italy	4.9	1.3	2.6	5.0	5.0	5.5	10.8	19.1	17.0
Spain	—	—	—	—	—	7.3	14.3	17.9	14.1

Inflation was fuelled by the cumulative effects of more than three decades of inflationary practices. It was amplified by the unbridled speculation of 1972 and 1973 in gold, land, buildings,

[15] McCracken report, op. cit., pp. 16–17, 275.

diamonds, jewels, works of art, and most of all, raw materials –
in short, all the 'real values' and 'refuge values' that appreciate
all the more as paper money depreciates. It was reinforced by
the practice of 'administered prices' imposed by the monopolies. It was accentuated by colossal military spending, which
is rising ceaselessly and to which all bourgeois societies have
become accustomed. (It is significant that among the innumerable denunciations of the 'factors responsible for inflation'
there is never any mention of the $250 thousand million in
annual military spending by the capitalist countries as a
whole!)[16]

The prime cause of inflation, however, is undeniably the
swelling of credit in the private sector, in other words the
swelling of bank debts, and of credit facilities, which was the
essential pillar of the long period of expansion that preceded
the acceleration of inflation. *The western economy sailed to
prosperity on a sea of debt*, the cumulative incidence of which
inevitably accelerated inflation, as is shown in Tables 10 and 11.

Table 10

Public and Private Debt in the United States
(in thousand of millions of current dollars)

Year	A: GNP	B: public debt	C: private debt	B as % of A	C as % of A
1946	208.5	269.4	153.4	129.4	73.6
1950	284.8	239.4	276.8	84.0	97.2
1955	398.0	269.8	392.2	67.8	98.5
1960	503.7	301.0	566.1	59.7	112.4
1965	684.9	367.6	870.4	53.7	127.1
1969	932.1	484.7	1,383.8	52.0	148.4
1973	1,294.9	598.4	1,947.8	46.6	150.4
1974	1,397.4	642.9	2,134.4	46.0	152.8

Source: Figures up to 1969: *Economic Report of the President*, February 1970.

Figures as of 1969: *Survey of Current Business*, July 1975.

[16] Particularly in the analysis of the causes of inflation presented in the
McCracken report, except as concerns the exceptional role of spending to
finance the war in Vietnam and the incidence of this spending on the inflation
rate in the United States.

Table 11

Public and Private Debt in West Germany
(in thousands of millions of current DM)

Year	A: GNP	B: public debt	C: private debt	B as % of A	C as % of A
1950	98.1	1.2	20.6	1.2	21.0
1955	181.4	7.0	63.3	3.8	34.9
1960	284.7	17.6	116.2	6.2	40.8
1965	460.4	49.5	259.3	10.8	56.3
1970	685.6	95.4	416.7	13.9	60.8
1975	1,043.6	220.6	656.4	21.1	66.0

Source: Winfried Wolf: '"Modell Deutschland" oder Klassencharakter der Krise', in Mandel and Wolf: *Ende der Krise oder Krise ohne Ende?*, p. 202.

Moreover, the recession was accompanied by a number of particular bottlenecks. Instances of shortages in some sectors coincided with the general glut of commodities. Such coincidence commonly occurs on the eve or at the beginning of an over-production crisis. That crisis always begins by breaking out in a few key sectors and then gradually spreads to all or most sectors of production.[17]

Thus, the recession began in 1974 in the automobile and construction industries. It then spread to textiles, electrical appliances, and building materials (glass, cement, bricks), and finally hit petrochemicals. The steel industry was still suffering shortages throughout the summer of 1974; then this branch was hit by the full force of the recession. The same is true of the wood and furniture industry.

On the other hand, in the sectors of machine-tools, coal, oil, and cereals, supply continued to lag behind demand throughout the first phase of the recession. Sugar, however, suffered a spectacular downturn (a 30% fall in price in the space of several weeks). Oil sales diminished in volume. Orders in telecommunications, which had been thought to be undergoing indefinite and constant expansion, were on the decline in both Europe and Japan.

[17] Karl Marx, *Theories of Surplus Value*, Progress Publishers, Moscow, 1968, vol. II, pp. 517ff.

The coincidence of the recession with a serious famine in the Sahel and other areas of the 'third world' had disastrous effects on the populations concerned. Nothing better confirms the irrational and inhuman character of the capitalist system than the fact that millions of men, women, and children are gravely undernourished and threatened by starvation while enormous resources in machines, raw materials, and labour power remain unused. If they were used, tractors, fertilizers, electric pumps, and irrigation canals could have been built to rapidly increase food production and feed the hungry. But that would require that production be regulated by physical need and not by profit.

A general crisis of over-production of commodities, of general over-abundance of capital relative to the possibilities of valorization (in other words, a crisis of over-capitalization or over-accumulation), means, in the final analysis, that the total mass of available surplus-value no longer guarantees that all capital will reap the anticipated rate of profit. Under a 'normal' capitalist economy – one abandoned to its own internal logic without deliberate attempts by bourgeois states to modify or correct conjunctural imbalances to a certain degree – this is always reflected in a fall in prices. Under a market economy that is functioning normally, this is what inevitably results when supply vastly exceeds demand. In reality, given a system of stable currency, such price declines express the advances in the productivity of labour achieved during the preceding phase of expansion. In other words, the decline in the average value of commodities reflects an augmentation of productivity which had been temporarily concealed by the fever of expansion.

Today's capitalist market economy, however, no longer functions in an entirely normal and autonomous fashion. For more than forty years now, all bourgeois governments have been systematically applying techniques of intervention into economic life, the overall result of which has been to inflate the money supply (paper money and bank money) more rapidly than the increase in the volume of material production. The result is a depreciation of all paper currencies, in other words, a climate of first 'creeping' and then 'generalized' inflation. 'Creeping' or even 'generalized' inflation, however, does not prevent price declines in given sectors at given moments. It is only in a climate of *galloping* inflation that *all* prices rise ceaselessly (although not necessarily at the same rate; the law of value continues to hold sway even here!). Completely depreciated money remains constantly in circulation. Nobody wants to hold on to it. Everyone feverishly exchanges it for commodities. Such was the climate in Germany in 1923 or 1945–47, as well as in the countries of West Europe under the German occupation during the Second World War.

We are not yet experiencing a situation of galloping inflation in the imperialist countries as a whole. Certain prices may thus decline, even appreciably, if there is a situation of overproduction and an absence of rigid monopolistic control of the market. This was initially the case for stock-market prices. During the 1974–75 recession they suffered their worst depression since 1940, or even 1931, as is shown in Table 12.

Table 12

Stock Exchange Price Indices[18]

Stock Exchange	1973 highest	1973 lowest	1974 highest	1974 lowest	18 December 1974
London	509.5	305.9	339.3	150.4	161.1
New York	1,051.7	788.3	891.7	577.6	603.5
Toronto	237.9	200.4	228.8	150.6	153.3
Tokyo	422.5	284.7	342.5	252.0	282.4
Hong Kong	1,775.0	423.9	481.9	150.1	163.3
Paris	98.9	70.7	85.1	47.8	49.4
Brussels	142.3	112.8	131.5	84.2	87.2
Frankfurt	120.7	85.0	93.2	79.5	85.5
Amsterdam	171.9	113.3	140.8	94.6	106.1
Milan	147.3	98.3	154.2	87.0	87.8
Stockholm	389.5	297.2	410.6	303.3	304.8

This was also the case for the prices of construction sites, at least in some countries in which real estate speculation had

[18] *The Economist*, 22 December 1973 and 21 December 1974. *The Economist's* index for the Frankfurt stock exchange was modified between 29 June and 6 July 1974. In this table we have recalculated the 1974 figures on the basis of the old index.

been particularly unbridled during the preceding phase. For instance, the prices of construction sites in Britain in the summer of 1974 were 40% lower than they had been in the summer of 1973. Many a real estate or real estate credit company was brought to ruin. Finally, such was the case for most raw materials, except food products, coal, and petroleum products, as is shown in Table 13.

Table 13

Indices of Industrial Raw Materials Prices
(100 = average 1952–56)

Raw material	June 1974	September 1974	December 1974	December 1974 December 1973
Coal and coke	394.1	389.9	434.5	0
Petroleum products	485.1	483.8	485.6	0
Fibres	172.3	148.0	128.9	− 17.7
Fur and leather	161.1	163.6	92.5	+ 3.5
Wood	338.7	331.1	326.0	− 5.5
Rubber	119.6	100.7	93.9	− 17.6
Iron and steel	322.5	302.8	65.2	− 31.7
Non-ferrous metals	321.1	242.4	10.2	− 39.9

Some raw materials prices dropped even more sharply. In mid-December 1974 copper was down 60% from its peak, reached in April 1974. Rubber, hit by the crisis in the automobile industry, suffered a fall in price of the order of 52%, cotton of the order of 57%, zinc of the order of 45%. Moreover, despite the general atmosphere of inflation, there were some no less spectacular price declines for certain products of manufacturing industries hit especially severely by excess capacity and/or current over-production and subject to heightened competition on the market.[19]

---

[19] The most striking example is quartz crystals and quartz watches. The price per crystal collapsed from $5 to $0.65 (*Business Week*, 28 November 1977). In other fields, such as clothing and shoes, the gap between so-called cheap products and so-called quality ones largely re-opened again. There are suits for 250FF, shoes for 25FF a pair, and shirts for 15FF.

4. The Rise in Oil Prices

The effect on the general economic cycle of the increase in the price of oil and the additional revenue obtained by the countries of the Organization of Petroleum Exporting Countries (OPEC) has been vastly exaggerated. There is even a persistent myth that this is the essential cause of the 1974–75 recession. Apart from the ideological or outright political functions of this claim, its illogical character is manifest. It also runs counter to all the conclusions of the theory of periodic crises (of the industrial cycle) under capitalism, whether in its Marxist or academic version.

There have been exactly twenty over-production crises since the formation of the world market, occurring at more or less regular intervals: 1825, 1836, 1847, 1857, 1866, 1873, 1882, 1891, 1900, 1907, 1913, 1921, 1929, 1937, 1949, 1953, 1958, 1961, 1970, and 1974–75. (In each case we have taken the date of the outbreak of the crisis in the capitalist country that dominated the world market at the time, Britain before the First World War and the United States thereafter; there was also a mini-crisis in the United States in 1966–67, but without an absolute decline in production.) To suppose that a malady that recurs twenty times has particular and unique causes on each occasion, causes not even related to the nature of the disease, 'political' causes, is plainly implausible and illogical.[20]

Some people have attempted to offer a pseudo-Keynesian version of the claim that the rises in oil prices were responsible for the 1974–75 recession. According to this theory, there was a 'transfer of resources' out of the industrialized countries, which caused a contraction of demand and production in those countries. Here again, there is an obvious error of reasoning. The factories laying workers off are not those producing for export. Since the world capitalist market constitutes a whole, a 'transfer of purchasing power' from West Europe, the United States, or Japan to the OPEC countries can have deflationary effects in the imperialist countries only to the extent that this purchasing power is sterile, not transformed into additional

---

[20] For example see Claasen and Lindbeck, op. cit., pp. 191–6.

demand for products and services imported from the industrialized countries.

But, it can be asked, does not at least that portion of the trade surpluses of the OPEC countries with respect to the rest of the capitalist countries which is 'hoarded' and unspent, reduce the 'aggregate demand' of the capitalist world? Apart from the fact that this hoarded portion is extremely small, representing at most some 1.5% of the GNP of the imperialist countries (and thus cannot possibly account for a recession of the scope of that of 1974–75, even in terms of its multiplier effect), the argument does not hold up even technically. In reality, genuine hoarding occurs only when these surpluses (the famous 'petrodollars') are actually withdrawn from the circuit 'commodities-paper money-credit money' which envelops the capitalist economy as a whole. Now, this occurs only if these petrodollars are hoarded in strongboxes in Riyadh, Kuwait, Tripoli, or Teheran in the form of gold, diamonds, or 'strong currencies'. But the immense majority of these petrodollar surpluses are actually placed in western banks in the form of short-term deposits. They are used by the imperialist banks to fuel their credit operations, to inflate the bank money supply. Paradoxically, it may be affirmed that far from having a deflationary effect on the imperialist economy, the balance of payments surpluses of the OPEC countries and the manner in which they have been used have maintained and extended the 'liquidity' of the international monetary system and thereby maintained the inflationary climate.[21]

The paradox, moreover, is merely apparent. The *real* incidence of the rise in oil prices on the economic cycle is twofold. On the one hand, by accentuating the general inflationary trend (both through augmenting costs and through amplifying liquidity), it advanced the moment at which inflation began to have negative effects on the conjuncture and at which governments were thus compelled to take measures to curb inflation to a certain extent. On the other hand, by weighing on the ·

[21] See the article 'Les liquidités internationales après le choc pétrolier' in the bulletin *Conjoncture* of the Société Générale (November 1977).

average rate of profit of industrial capital, it accentuated the downward movement of that rate of profit, which was the fundamental cause of the recession.

In both cases, however, it is a question of intensifying trends that were already under way. The generalized recession was already inherent in the cycle that began with the still-partial recession of 1970–71 and continued into the speculative boom of 1972–73. Constantly rising excess production capacities and runaway inflation incontestably attest to this. Now, these two movements preceded the quadrupling of oil prices by the OPEC countries in the wake of the October War of 1973. The rise in oil prices was thus neither the cause nor even the immediate detonator of the recession. It was, at most, an additional factor exacerbating the gravity of the crisis.

It is true that the preceding argument treats the international capitalist economy as a whole, which it undeniably is. But it is a whole *structured into 'national' states and markets.* Some countries, both imperialist and semi-colonial, suffered from the sharp rise in oil prices much more than others. Japan, which had an enormous balance of payments deficit in 1973 as a result of the increase in oil prices, was able to absorb this deficit through a spectacular upsurge of its exports. The same is true of West Germany, and up to 1976 it was true of the United States too. Other countries were hit to the maximum extent and they indeed did suffer deflationary effects, either because they had to reduce imports of energy and raw materials in order to reduce their enormous balance of payments deficits or because they were led to apply a policy of general deflation of credit and demand in order to try to absorb the deficit. In these cases the indirect effects of the oil price increases did contribute to precipitating the recession.

But it must be emphasized that without exception this applies only to countries that are in no way decisive in determining the international economic situation. In the countries that *are* decisive – primarily the United States, Japan, and West Germany – the turn in the industrial cycle in 1974 can in no way be ascribed to the direct or indirect incidence of the oil price increases. Or better: those countries which suffered most from these increases – particularly Britain and Italy – remained in a state of recession in 1977, even though recovery of the international capitalist economy had been under way for two years. Thus, there is no cause and effect relation between the increase in oil prices and the reversal of the cycle in 1974–75.

We may add that even in countries like Britain, Italy, and to some extent, France where the oil price rises seem to have compelled governments to apply a pronounced deflationary policy, the cause and effect relation is mediated by the *political and social options of the incumbent governments*. It is not true that a deflationary policy was the only option technically possible under the given circumstances. Other variants of economic and monetary policy were available. If they were not adopted, it was for reasons of socio-political preference, the class nature of which must be exposed, and not because it was technically impossible to seek another road.

There has, moreover, been a tendency strongly to exaggerate the accumulation of exchange reserves by the oil exporting countries in 1973–74. Imperialist circles unleashed consciously alarmist propaganda in this regard. The World Bank had initially advanced the fantastic figure of a short-term accumulation of $650 thousand million in the coffers of the member countries of OPEC. Studies undertaken by the Brookings Institution and the Morgan Guarantee Trust Company later revised these estimates downward, predicting that the maximum exchange-reserve holdings of the OPEC countries would be $280 thousand million in 1978, a figure which was expected to decline to $179 thousand million by 1980. (All these estimates were based on a dollar exchange rate remaining more or less stable at the 1974 level.) Since then these figures have once again been revised downward.

The reason for this revision is not difficult to discover. All the OPEC countries immediately saw the new currency resources accumulated through the increases in oil prices as a means to initiate or accelerate economic development plans that would enable them to extricate themselves definitively from underdevelopment. For the ruling classes in these countries this would entail at once reduced risks of social explosion and a greater opportunity to accumulate capital on a massive scale.

The majority of the OPEC countries are relatively densely populated. Even resources as great as those generated by the quadrupling of oil prices do not suffice to sustain a long-term process of accelerated industrialization in these countries. They thus quickly found themselves with balance of payments deficits resulting from the huge volume of imports required to support grandiose development plans. This was particularly the case for Nigeria, Algeria, Iran, Iraq, and Venezuela, not to mention Indonesia. Under these conditions, only the countries with much lower population densities – primarily Saudi Arabia, Kuwait, the United Arab Emirates, and Qatar, Libya constituting an intermediary case – were able to maintain continuous balance of payments surpluses. The overall impact of these surpluses on the international capitalist economy was mitigated by the reappearance of heavy deficits in the first category of OPEC countries.[22]

It had been estimated that the overall balance of payments surpluses of the oil exporting countries would total $80 thousand million in 1975. In fact the figure was only $57 thousand million. (Subsequently, these surpluses have continued to shrink. According to the Bank of England, they were $36 thousand million in 1976 and $33 thousand million in 1977, of which $20.8 thousand million was accumulated during the first half of the year and only $12.2 thousand million during the second half.) And it must be added that this $57 thousand million surplus corresponds to a cumulative balance of payments deficit in the imperialist countries (members of the OECD) of only $30–35 thousand million, the remainder representing the accumulated deficit of the semi-colonial and dependent capitalist countries and the so-called socialist countries. Since the *trade balance* of the OPEC countries showed a surplus of $97 thousand million in 1974, it is apparent that these countries spent some $40 thousand million abroad in one form or another.

[22] In this regard see the interesting study by Amin Maalouf in the monthly magazine *Economia*, Paris, March 1977.

Even during the preceding year, 1973, some $60 thousand
million in petrodollars had been spent abroad. In 1974 these
investments rose to $57 thousand million. They were divided in
the following manner:

43.0%   Euro-money markets (including Euro-dollars);
20.7%   long-term investments in countries other than the
        United States and Britain;
12.2%   long-term investments in the United States (includ-
        ing state securities);
7.7%   short-term investments in Britain (including
        treasury bonds);
7.0%   short-term investments in the United States (includ-
        ing treasury bonds);
6.0%   deposits in international organizations;
2.7%   long-term investments in Britain (including state
        securities).[23]

The repercussions of the fall in the balance of payments
surpluses of the OPEC countries seriously disrupted Britain's
balance of payments, for it led to massive withdrawals of
petrodollars that had been deposited in British banks in 1973
and 1974.

5. The Semi-Colonial and Dependent Countries

In examining the effects of the recession and the rise in oil
prices on the economy of the so-called third world – more
accurately: the semi-colonial and dependent capitalist countries – the case of the oil-exporting countries must be sharply
distinguished from that of the rest of the 'third world'. The
considerable revenues obtained by the first category of countries effectively protected them from the direct and indirect
effects of the recession. The oil cartel 'held together' despite

[23] Bank for International Settlements, *47e Rapport Annuel*, Basle, 13 June
1977, p. 101, according to the calculations of the Bank of England and the
Supplément à l'Etude sur l'Economie mondiale 1975 (United Nations, New York,
1977, p. 329). For 1975 the BIS report gives the figure of $36 thousand million
invested abroad by OPEC members, while the UN supplement cites the figure
of $31 thousand million.

the recession, and the fall in the demand for and volume of exports.[24] The size of the oil income of the owning classes of the OPEC countries is represented in Table 14. About half this

Table 14

Oil Revenues of the OPEC Countries in 1974
(estimates in millions of current dollars)

Saudi Arabia	$29,500
Iran	21,000
Venezuela	10,600
Nigeria	9,233
Kuwait	9,000
Libya	9,000
Iraq	7,000
Abu Dhabi	5,300
Algeria	5,000
Total OPEC:	$\pm$ 110 thousand million

sum was devoted to increasing imports, of capital goods (for the infrastructure, industry, and agriculture) as well as consumer goods.

The capitalization of the oil income, the accumulation of enormous money-capital both in the hands of the state (although in many OPEC countries the state is the 'property' of a few private families) and in the hands of the ruling class, inevitably leads to the more or less pronounced beginning of a process of industrialization, of accumulation of industrial capital and the formation of an 'indigenous' finance capital on a grand scale. Further on, we shall examine the incidence of this feverish drive to accumulate capital in the relatively 'new' capitalist countries on the overall structure of the world market.[25]

In the long run, the industrialization of the OPEC countries

[24] In their attempts to 'hold' the cartel price, nearly all OPEC countries had to make significant reductions in production during the recession.

[25] 'Those who have studied the conflicting petrochemical development projects of Saudi Arabia, Kuwait, and Iran for the coming decade believe that there are chances of cut-throat competition for markets among factories that will be producing essentially similar products (not to mention Qatar's entrance into the domain of over-production)', *The Economist*, 10 December 1977.

will accentuate the internal contradictions of the economy of the imperialist countries, since it will inevitably extend and aggravate phenomena of excess production capacity in a whole series of industrial branches. *In the short run*, it creates additional outlets for those industrial branches in the imperialist countries which specialize in the export of capital goods and infrastructural equipment: the construction of 'ready-made' factories, public works projects, and so on.[26] Here are some of the most important projects announced during the 1974–75 recession:

– A joint venture between Iran and the American chemical trust Dupont de Nemours, estimated value $280 million;

– A joint venture between Iran and the German trust Thyssen for the establishment of a steel factory and two brick-making factories in Ahvaz and Isfahan;

– A joint venture between Iran, the Thyssen trust, and the American Fluor Corporation of Los Angeles for construction of a new oil refinery in Abadan;

– The construction of a new industrial metropolis in al-Jubail, Saudi Arabia, including, among other things, an oil refinery and several petrochemical complexes;

– The creation of an enormous synthetic fertilizer factory in Iraq.

These are only a few examples among many.[27]

It follows that exports of machinery, capital goods, and 'ready-made factories' will occupy an increasingly important place in world trade in the future. The exports of this branch of Japanese industry rose from $1.5 thousand million in 1972 to $3 thousand million in 1974.[28] It is considered the most expansive and dynamic sector of the Japanese economy, one which merits special protection from the government.

It also follows, however, that the OPEC countries will

[26] In my *Marxist Economic Theory*, London, 1968, vol. II, pp. 480–81, I indicated the reasons why the most powerful monopolies in the imperialist countries were modifying their attitude towards the industrialization of the 'third world' and were beginning to foster it to some extent.

[27] *Business Week*, 26 May 1975.

[28] *Far Eastern Economic Review*, 16 May 1975.

acquire greater importance as markets for the imperialist countries, even though their share of the total exports of these countries remains modest. In the case of West Germany and Japan, this increased share is already clearly indicated by current statistics (see below, pp. 130–1). It is interesting to note that French exports to Algeria have nearly tripled over three years, rising from 2.38 thousand million francs in 1972 to 6.2 thousand million francs in 1974.

Nevertheless, 'optimistic' projections which regard the accumulation of currency in the hands of the possessing classes of the OPEC countries purely as creating additional outlets for the international imperialist economy and therefore as the motor force of a new phase of expansion are vitiated by four important errors:

(1) The dynamic of oil sales and prices, which determines the import capacities of the OPEC countries, remains highly uncertain. It is already clear that a portion of the gains of the possessing classes of these countries are and will be wiped out by rising prices of imported products on the one hand and by the devaluation of the dollar and the pound sterling on the other hand. (The latter factor affects the portion of this income preserved in liquid or semi-liquid form.) In demanding that oil prices be indexed to the prices of manufactured products or that they be registered in Special Drawing Rights (international money of account apparently 'guaranteed' against devaluation), the OPEC countries are seeking to escape this infernal logic of the international capitalist economy, which continues to be dominated by imperialism. But SDRs are merely money of account. One can be paid only in current paper money, and not in 'paper-gold'. Any conversion of SDRs into dollars, or into other currencies suffering from inexorable and constant depreciation, would thus touch off compensating mechanisms: an even more pronounced fall of the dollar; an even more pronounced reduction of the relative consumption of oil;[29] a more

[29] The physical consumption of hydrocarbons in West Europe declined 6.6% in 1975 and 5.1% in 1975. The equivalent percentages for Japan were 3.8% and 5.8%, for the United States and Canada 3.8% and 2.1% (GATT, *Le commerce international en 1976/77*, Geneva, 1977, p. 69).

feverish search for alternative energy sources; an even stronger rise in the prices of the capital goods exported to the OPEC countries. Any of these factors would threaten to neutralize the long- and short-term advantages of posting prices in SDRs.

(2) The OPEC increases in oil prices will touch off a progressive substitution, over a protracted period, of energy sources not exported by the members of the cartel (including oil from other sources). Experts estimate that over-production of oil and excess capacity of refineries will persist until 1982. OPEC's share in world oil production will decline from today's 60% to 40% in 1985 if OPEC members continue to index their sales price to the world inflation rate.[30]

(3) The cumulative industrialization of the OPEC countries is contradicted by their retrograde socio-economic structure, the lack of a real agrarian revolution in the densely populated countries, the shortage of labour in the less densely populated countries, the aggravation of class contradictions that will inevitably be stimulated by accelerated inflation in nearly all cases, the uprooting of the rural population, and the super-exploitation of the proletariat. This cumulative industrialization thus threatens to halt at a certain threshold.

(4) The average growth rate of the international capitalist economy as a whole is neither an 'external' nor 'unimportant' element in determining the impact of the industrialization of the OPEC countries on the economy of the imperialist countries. As we have already emphasized, to the extent that we have now entered a 'long wave' of extremely sluggish growth, any leap forward in the industrial productive capacity existing in the OPEC countries threatens seriously to aggravate the crisis of important industrial sectors in the imperialist countries, above all refineries, petrochemicals, the steel industry, and the synthetic fertilizer industry.

---

[30] *Business Week*, 16 January 1978. 'Although most experts estimate that there will be a world oil and gas shortage in a few years, this will certainly not happen in 1978. For most American oil producers, 1978 will be a repetition of 1977. Their major problem will be a colossal excess of oil and petroleum products', *Business Week*, 9 January 1978. Oil refineries in capitalist Europe worked at only 63% capacity in 1977.

In any event, although 'black gold' did enable the OPEC countries to escape the immediate effects of the international recession on their own economies, they nonetheless constitute an exception in this respect among the semi-colonial and dependent countries as a whole. For the rest of these countries, the conjunction of the rise in oil prices, the international economic recession, and food shortages, which persisted throughout 1974, struck them more cruelly than they had been struck at any time since the collapse of the Korean war boom.[31] Countries like Pakistan, Bangladesh, most of the countries of East and Equatorial Africa, and several Latin American countries which have no oil, were struck simultaneously in a four-fold fashion:

(a) The rise in the price of oil significantly aggravated their already chronic balance of payments deficits and absorbed a good part, if not all, of the 'aid' they received, thus retarding or halting important projects, particularly those related to the modernization of agriculture.

(b) The rise in the price of the foodstuffs and chemical fertilizers they have to import from the world market cost them even more than the rise in oil prices. The cost of the food and fertilizer imports of the semi-colonial and dependent countries increased $5 thousand million in 1973. In 1974 it increased by a similar amount. The cost of their oil imports rose only $1–2 thousand million in 1973 and $7 thousand million in 1974, for a total of $8 thousand million during those two years, as opposed to $10 thousand million for imports of food and fertilizers.

(c) The price collapse of a whole series of raw materials and the reduction in the volume of their industrial exports as a

---

[31] In an article published in *Le Monde Diplomatique* (September 1975) under the title 'Détérioration des termes d'échange et "désaccumulation" du capital' Frédéric F. Clairmonte recalled that the terms of trade for basic products had deteriorated from an index of 126 in 1953 to an index of 84 in 1972 (and from 138 to 84 from 1954 to 1972), according to the statistics of UNCTAD. The annual losses thus suffered by the 'third world' countries amount to thousands of millions of dollars ($10 thousand million in 1972 alone). This situation was turned around by the spectacular rise in oil prices in 1973 and 1974. But this seems to have been partially neutralized already by the new decline in the prices of many raw materials in 1975 and again in 1977.

result of the effects of the international recession diminished their exchange reserves at the very moment that their expenses had risen considerably because of the increase in the price of imports.[32]

(d) The cumulative effects of all these factors provoked a regression in the productivity of labour in agriculture, combined in several cases with a decline in absolute production and a stagnation, or even decline, in industrial production (because it was impossible to maintain the necessary level of imports of certain raw materials and spare parts, since demand on the domestic market declined, as did exports, etc.).

Parts of the Indian subcontinent suffered catastrophe, as did the countries of the Sahel. According to an estimate of the Morgan Guarantee Trust Company, the semi-colonial and dependent countries that do not export oil registered the following balance of payments deficits in 1974:

Table 15

Balance of Payments Deficits of Semi-Colonial and Dependent Countries in 1974 (in millions of dollars)

Brazil	7,000
Mexico	2,500
India	1,800
South Korea	1,800
Taiwan	1,200
Peru	850
Kenya	450
Chile	434
Turkey	400
Argentina	352
Philippines	290
Thailand	150
Zambia	100
Malaysia	100

According to the International Monetary Fund, the total balance of payments deficit of the under-developed countries

[32] In 1975 the underdeveloped countries that do not export oil suffered a 5% decline in the volume of their exports, a 12% decline in the value of their exports, and a 5.5% decline in their exchange reserves (United Nations, *Supplément à l'Etude sur l'Economie mondiale 1975*, p. 278).

that do not export oil reached $30 thousand million in 1974, $28 thousand million in 1975, and $25 thousand million in 1976. The estimate for 1977 is $25 thousand million.

These deficits were partially neutralized by an influx of bank loans (and to a lesser extent of loans from international public institutions). Further on we shall deal with the significance and consequences of this additional debt. For the moment, let us simply register this conclusion: any capitalist over-production crisis strikes the weak more harshly than the strong, the poor more harshly than the rich. This is true within the imperialist countries themselves, as the crisis affects the proletariat and the bourgeoisie. It is true within the employer class vis-à-vis the small and middle-sized companies on the one hand and the great monopolies on the other. And it is true on a world scale, vis-à-vis the semi-colonial and dependent countries on the one hand and the imperialist countries on the other.

2

Industrial Contraction, Financial Panic

1. Inter-Imperialist Competition

Inter-imperialist competition always tends to sharpen when the economic cycle is in a downturn. This is the time when 'sacred egotism' gains the upper hand. Each 'national' capitalist class seeks in the first instance to save itself, exporting its difficulties and unemployment to its neighbours and competitors. The imperialist bourgeoisie of the United States had lost its *absolute* hegemony over the capitalist world, acquired in 1945, during the sixties, which were marked by a spectacular new rise of West European (especially West German) and Japanese imperialism. Towards the end of the sixties the American bourgeoisie sought to react. The first step was the devaluation of the dollar (leading inevitably to the end of its convertibility for gold), the aim of which was to bolster the competitive position of the American bourgeoisie on the world market. The U.S. bourgeoisie then saw the increase in the price of oil as an excellent opportunity to strike back at its European and Japanese competitors, who had enjoyed lower energy prices during the sixties but were more dependent on oil imports than the United States. (Both these manoeuvres backfired, as we shall have occasion to see further on.)

There is no disputing that at the beginning of the 1974–75 recession the *relative* hegemony of American imperialism over the capitalist world seemed more certain than several years earlier.[1] Was this still true after the recession, in the midst of

[1] In regard to the rise in oil prices, J. P. Chevènement wrote in his otherwise highly interesting book *Le Vieux, la Crise et le Neuf* (Flammarion, Paris, 1974):

the recovery? The least one can say is that the question has yet to be settled. As far as international trade is concerned, 1974 and 1975 saw a sensational counteroffensive by West German and Japanese exports, which further reduced the share of American manufactured products on the world market of goods produced by transformation industry. The relatively stable condition of American exports *as a whole* results from the fact that these exports include a fair number of raw materials and, particularly, a significant proportion of food products, which benefited from price increases and heightened demand in 1974 and at the beginning of 1975; such classes of products constitute a negligible or even non-existent portion of West German and Japanese exports.

In 1974 West German exports exceeded those of the United States, even in absolute figures, for the first time. While this was exceptional, the fact that the West German manufacturing industry now holds first place in the world market for products of this sector seems a much more lasting phenomenon. (In this regard, see Table 23. Table 16 indicates the situation for exports as a whole.)

Table 16

Exports at Annual Rate, in Value (in thousands of millions of current dollars)

Country	1970	1973	1974	1975	1976	1977
United States	43.2	71.3	98.5	108.0	114.7	122.1
West Germany	34.2	67.5	92.6	92.8	99.2	113.1
Japan	19.3	37.0	55.5	55.1	66.0	79.1
France	18.1	36.7	50.0	52.7	54.5	69.9
Britain	19.3	30.5	36.5	41.5	45.7	64.0
Italy	13.2	22.2	27.0	33.7	39.8	46.0
Canada	16.8	26.3	37.5	33.5	40.1	—
Netherlands	11.8	24.1	31.5	30.5	32.8	40.8
Belgium	11.6	22.5	27.6	27.0	36.7	48.5

'Japanese and European balances of payments suddenly went into deficit, while the United States reestablished its trade balance'. We know what happened later. Chevènement's mistake was made by most observers at the time.

The position of the four major imperialist powers did not change substantially. Nevertheless, account must be taken of the important currency modifications that had occurred since 1970, including a significant depreciation of the dollar and a strong appreciation of the deutschmark. Because of these changes, the evolution of the *volume* of exports is not reflected in the figures in Table 16. It is also important to note the very heavy decline in the position of Britain, whose exports equalled those of Japan in 1970 but were 20% lower than Japan's in 1975, and the relatively good showing of French exports (lower than those of Britain and the Benelux countries in 1970, 20% higher than those of Britain in 1975, nearly equalling those of the Benelux countries). Italian exports stood up better than predicted, while Canada lost ground.

To those who claim that these comparisons suffer from an unwarranted identification of 'various capitals' with 'territoriality',[2] we reply that the comparison is equally striking, if not more so, if we measure the performance of the great multinational corporations, whether American, Japanese, or of European inclination. To see this it is sufficient to compare the dynamic of the capital exports and industrial initiatives of these three categories of 'multinationals' throughout the world during the years 1974, 1975, 1976, and 1977. The reason for this is hardly mysterious. American big capital has not succeeded in containing the advances in productivity, and thereby the successes on the world market, of West Germany and Japan.

In 1959 the world's largest firm in eleven of the thirteen major branches of industrial manufacturing and banking was American; by 1974 this was the case in only seven branches. In 1959 some 63% of the 156 largest firms in these thirteen branches were American; by 1974 the percentage had declined to 43%, as against 36.5% for the European multinationals and 20% for the

---

[2] Cf. Chr. Palloix, *L'Economie mondiale capitaliste*, vol. II, Maspero, Paris, 1972. The reality and scope of inter-imperialist competition and of the strength of the European and Japanese multinationals eluded several of the authors who contributed to the collection *Ruptures d'un système économique* (Dunod, Paris, 1978). Dockes and Rosier even speak of a 'vassalization' of Germany and Japan with respect to the United States, although the fundamental trend is clearly in the opposite direction.

Japanese multinationals. In 1977, 22 of the world's 50 largest firms were American, 21 were European, 5 were Japanese, and 2 were Latin American. Of the world's 20 largest banks at the end of 1976, 10 were European, only 4 were American (although admittedly American banks held the first, second, and fourth position), 5 were Japanese, and one was Brazilian.[3]

As for the monetary system, the U.S. imperialist project of ending the gold standard and definitively institutionalizing a dollar not convertible into gold as the basis of a new international monetary system founded on SDRs (special drawing rights) has even less chance of gaining lasting acceptance than it did in the past. The more inflation spreads and lasts, the less owners of commodities and holders of debts can *be compelled* to accept unconvertible paper money whose value is plunging.[4] In the final analysis, a world paper money imposed on all capitalists as a means of exchange and payment that could not be legally refused presupposes a world state, a world government, and this means the disappearance of inter-imperialist competition, i.e. super-imperialism. And we are further from that than ever.

It is on the politico-military plane that the predominance of American imperialism remains most pronounced, despite its heavy defeat in Indochina. This predominance is clearly not a function of its relative decline in the economic, financial, and monetary domain but is in clear contradiction with it. The inability of the European bourgeoisie to achieve new advances in monetary and political integration within the Common Market,[5] to transform it from a confederation of states into a federal state consolidating the politico-military status quo, has

[3] *Le Monde, L'Année économique et sociale 1977*, p. 12; *The Economist*, 4 February 1978, p. 78.

[4] 'Whereas in the past it was practically zero, nearly 20% of Japanese exports are now paid for in yen. Although this is still the situation for West Germany, which finances more than 70% of its trade in DM, the rise of financing (of exports) in yen is transforming the yen into a currency commonly accepted throughout the world', *Business Week*, 11 April 1977. 'Many foreigners are asking American companies to bill them in currencies other than the dollar', *Business Week*, 26 December 1977.

[5] See the plea in favour of a European currency in Bernard Schmid, *La Monnaie européenne*, Paris, 1977.

cost the European bourgeoisie dearly, even financially. Its internal contradictions are deeply felt, as are those of Japanese imperialism. These threaten to impose additional burdens, and the European bourgeoisie may well have to bear the costs of some spectacular trade modifications. Such factors, when thrown into the scales opposite the slower rise of industrial productivity in the United States, generally maintain the present balance of forces.

Since the capitalist world as a whole has escaped American 'leadership' without being able to replace it with an alliance based on an equality of power among the United States, Japan, and the European powers, or with some other force commanding hegemony, the capitalist world is suffering a *crisis of international political leadership* even more sharply now than in previous years. There is no reason whatever to suppose that decisive changes in this regard will occur in coming months and years.

2. The Major Branches of Industry

An assessment of the longer-term effects of the 1974–75 recession on the international capitalist economy must include an analysis of the situation of the major branches of industry: the degree of excess capacity at present and in the long run, the extent of over-production, the varying rates of recession they suffered, and the sort of recovery they can expect.

The automobile industry was the industrial branch that essentially 'generated' the long period of post-war expansion in the imperialist countries. It was also the branch, along with the construction industry, that 'triggered' the 1974–75 recession. Then it again played a 'detonating' role in stimulating the recovery of 1976–77 in the United States, Japan, and West Germany. The extent of the reduction in production in 1974–75 varied from 25–36% in all the major producing countries, except Japan, where it was limited to 7%. Even the Brazilian automobile industry, which was still able to expand production 17.5% in 1974 (while the Argentine auto industry suffered a 10% decline), was compelled to reduce its rate of activity in 1975 and 1976.

Lasting excess capacity now exists on a world scale, although its scope remains to be determined (it can be estimated as between 10% and 20%). New demand seems largely saturated, except in some dependent countries and in the so-called socialist countries. Current demand is largely a replacement demand, and the rate of expansion for the industry is generally modest.[6] Obviously, strong conjunctural booms, following in the wake of violent sales reductions, remain possible within this general context. Such a boom undoubtedly occurred in 1976 and at the beginning of 1977. Even the substitution demand obviously remains considerable.

But it is nevertheless clear that the existence of excess capacity on a world scale, combined with the establishment of many new production centres in the dependent countries, will force a restructuring of this industry during the next few years. Some of the weakest of the big firms (British Leyland, Volvo, Citroën, Chrysler, the weakest of the Japanese firms) are probably condemned in the long run either to disappear or to be absorbed by one of the multinationals that can better resist the storm of recession and restructuring.

The *construction industry* was the branch, along with the automobile industry (in some countries even more than the automobile industry), that was hardest hit by the 1974–75 recession, particularly as a consequence of the policy of credit restriction universally applied in 1973–74 and of the decline in real consumer incomes. These factors, combined with a dizzying increase in the price of materials and building sites, completely disrupted the market in housing – not to mention factory construction, which was hit by the plunge of productive investment. The evolution of investment in housing construction is indicated in Table 17.

The number of construction starts in the United States fell *by nearly half*, from an annual level of 1,880,000 in February 1974 to an annual level of 990,000 in April 1975. And these figures ought to be compared with the record level attained

---

[6] *Business Week* (9 January 1978) speaks of a virtual saturation of demand for the automobile industry in the United States.

before the outbreak of the recession, at the beginning of 1973 (an annual rate of 2.5 million construction starts). The recovery in construction, slow at first, accelerated only during 1977. In December 1977 the annual rate of construction starts had risen to 2.2 million, still below the record level of 1973. Here again, the market seems clearly saturated.

In Japan and West Europe, where the housing shortage is more pronounced in some countries, long-term prospects seem less uncertain, although stagnation has persisted since the beginning of the recession (housing starts in Japan during the first quarter of 1977 were 25% lower than during the last quarter of 1973). But inflation will inevitably exercise a twofold pressure, on the one hand raising prices for materials and building sites and on the other hand making credit more expensive (and this will be combined with a more restrictive credit policy). This makes a new boom in the construction industry unlikely in the years immediately ahead.

Closely linked to the construction industry, the *electrical appliance industry* suffered a genuine slump in 1974–75, comparable to the recession in the automobile industry. In January

Table 17

Evolution of Spending on Residential Investment
(rate of annual variation, as % of GNP)

Country	Average 1962–73	1974	1975
West Germany	+ 3.5	− 8.7	− 9.0
Belgium	+ 4.5	+10.2	− 6.1
Canada	+ 6.8	− 2.0	− 7.7
Spain	+ 9.3	+ 4.4	− 3.5
United States	+ 4.2	−27.8	−16.3
France	+ 7.8	+ 4.9	− 3.9
Italy	+ 2.2	+ 2.6	−11.6
Japan	+15.1	−11.2	+ 7.9
Netherlands	+ 9.3	−13.7	− 7.1
Britain	+ 3.5	− 2.5	+ 6.6
Switzerland	+ 5.3	−17.4	−39.3

Source: Bank for International Settlements, *47e Rapport Annuel*, Basle, 13 June 1977, p. 19.

1975 sales in this branch in the United States were 39% lower than in January 1974. The decline was of the order of 13.4% for 1974 as a whole compared with 1973. It was smaller in the nine Common Market countries, about 7%. It must nevertheless be noted that between 1974 and 1975 production of refrigerators, washing machines, and smaller household appliances declined more than 10% in the Common Market countries.

It is difficult to assess the degree of long-term excess capacity in this sector, characterized by growing saturation of the market for 'old products', continuing technological innovation, and appreciable difficulties in 'generating' new needs. Nevertheless, because of its 'coupling' with the construction industry, it would be difficult for this branch to recover the growth rates of the sixties. A strong expansion of investments in this sector is therefore unlikely.

The *textile industry* also suffered disproportionately in the recession, although in varying degrees. The crisis in the textile industry was especially severe in West Europe, Japan, and Brazil. In Britain it was reported that 150,000 of the 830,000 workers employed by this industry were on short time as of mid-March 1975. In Brazil, where total textile production (cloth and clothing in natural fibres and synthetics) had increased from 750,000 tonnes in 1970 to 1.1 million tonnes in 1974 (with an expansion of exports from 390,000 million tonnes in 1970 to 500,000 million tonnes in 1974), exports during the first quarter of 1975 were down 50% from the first quarter of 1974. Some 5% of the work force in textiles was laid off and investments fell by two-thirds. This trend continued in 1976–77, in spite of a slight upturn of exports. The employment index for textiles in Sao Paulo fell by a third between October 1976 and March 1977. The two largest Japanese textile trusts were working at only 60% capacity during the first quarter of 1975. Total production of textiles fell 8% from 1974 to 1975 in the nine EEC countries, but there were strong disparities among countries and sub-branches.

In this industry as well, there can be no question of an overall expansion of investments in the long run or of a growing share of world exports (or production). On the contrary, the share of total consumer spending devoted to clothing will tend to diminish or, in the best of cases, to stagnate. Investments will probably be for the most part rationalization investments, and the advances in some countries will result primarily from substitution of products (compensated by declines in exports or even in production in other countries).[7]

The *petrochemicals industry* is marked by a cycle of its own (probably quadrennial), and the shift from conditions of relative shortage, provoked primarily by speculative inventory building consequent to the rise in oil prices in 1973, to conditions of over-production and price collapse was particularly rapid during 1974. The price of polyester thread fell from $1.30 to $0.86 a pound. Declines in production and sales seemed to bottom out in January and February 1975. In West Germany, Italy, and France production was of the order of 20% lower in 1975 than in 1974. Since then there has been a certain recovery due to inventory utilization. The price of polyester thread has risen to $1.05 a pound. The capitalists of this industry, which still enjoys an expanding long-term demand, are hoping for a real and lasting upturn. But the phenomenon of excess capacity is quite pronounced in this industry. The establishment of powerful production centres in some of the dependent countries will probably provoke cut-throat competition and a worldwide restructuring of production capacities. In July 1977 the EEC Commission sent a letter to the nine member governments asking them to cease according financial aid to new investments but rather to encourage a reduction in productive capacity. With the agreement of the trusts in this sector, a 15% reduction in production, or 450,000 tonnes, is planned in the EEC countries between 1978 and 1981.

For the *chemicals industry in general* a distinction must be made between the various sub-sectors. The expansion of the pharmaceutical industry is expected to continue, barring political and social upheavals. (The particularly scandalous manner in which this industry profits from the social security

---

[7] See Chapter Four. Even in Brazil investment in the textile industry is in clear decline, cf. *Gazeta Mercantil*, July 1977.

systems in the imperialist countries and over-charges for its products in the semi-colonial and dependent countries makes it highly vulnerable to demands for state intervention, including the demand for nationalization, raised by public opinion among the working class and even reformist and liberal public opinion.) On the other hand, the chemical fertilizer industry, which could have been expected to benefit from a world-wide effort to increase agricultural yields, has fallen into an apparently chronic situation of excess capacity. Prices 'exploded' during the period of shortage in 1973 and 1974, particularly doubling in the case of phosphates and nitrates. Even though sales had continued to rise, albeit at a slower rate (some 3–4% from July 1974 to July 1975 for the American industry, some 5% for nitrogenous fertilizers in West Europe), world market prices began to fall. The exceptional harvest in the United States provoked a decline in agricultural prices and the incomes of farmers, who reduced their purchases in 1976. There was a similar development in capitalist Europe, with production declines of the order of 15–20% for phosphates and nitrates in 1976. Here again we are dealing with a sector for which future demand, rapidly expanding in the semi-colonial and dependent countries, will tend increasingly to be satisfied by new installations constructed in the oil producing countries. For the chemical branch as a whole, the decline in production in the EEC countries was of the order of 10% in 1975, with a recovery of the same order in 1976.

The *steel industry*: the steel boom ended during the second half of 1974. The steel industry, like the petrochemical and textile industries, has experienced a cycle of its own during past decades which does not entirely coincide with that of industry as a whole. Orders for steel products in Western Europe during the first quarter of 1975 were down 33% from the first quarter of 1974. In April 1975 steel production in the capitalist countries as a whole was down 9.8% compared with the April 1974 level. The decline was 14.5% in the United States and Japan and 12.4% for the EEC countries (but more than 30% for Belgium and Portugal). Prices fell between 40% and 50% from November 1974 to March 1975. A new plunge into recession in the steel industry during autumn 1976 exacerbated this downward movement.

The 1975 recession in steel was manifestly the combined consequence of the crises of the automobile, construction, and shipbuilding industries, which are big customers of the steel industry. But the long-term optimism which the capitalists in this sector continue to exhibit ill masks a problem of lasting excess capacity, fuelled in particular by the rise of the steel industry in several dependent countries (Brazil, South Korea) and by the effort of modernization the American steel industry is now beginning to undertake so as to close its significant technological gap with respect to the Japanese and European industries.

Shipbuilding and aeronautics were particularly hard hit by the 1974–75 recession, for many reasons. The forecasts of continuing expansion in oil sales, founded on extrapolations of the trends of the sixties, had been the source of more or less significant tanker orders from the oil giants. But the fall in oil sales immobilized a portion of the existing tanker fleet (243 tankers with a total displacement of 13.5 million tonnes as of mid-March 1975), and this led to considerable losses for some firms (note the financial catastrophe of Burma Oil). The result was a massive reduction in orders.

More generally, the sharp contraction of world trade as a whole also had effects on freight levels and therefore on the volume of current shipbuilding. In the middle of 1975 some 10% of the world merchant fleet (including tankers) was immobile, and this percentage declined only slightly in 1976. From the beginning of the recession to mid-March 1975 some 20 million tonnes of construction orders were cancelled, which represents a total of about 7% of the shipbuilding capacity of the international capitalist economy as a whole. Japan, the Scandinavian countries, and the United States were especially hard hit.

The anarchy of capitalist production is strikingly manifested in the fact that throughout the period during which the volume of world sea trade was on the decline, the supply of cargo-space continued to rise. In 1975 the volume of world sea trade diminished by about 8% while the tonnage of the world merchant fleet rose 8%, from 312 million tonnes BRT to 342 million tonnes. As far as tankers are concerned, the discrepancy was even more striking. The volume of oil transported dropped 11%, but the tonnage of available tankers rose 15%.

It is not astonishing that under these conditions the amount of freight shipped began to diminish rapidly. For tankers, the index of freight for West Germany declined from 340 in October 1973 (the highest level reached) to 140 in January 1974, less than 100 in the middle of 1974, and 60 in March 1975 (the lowest level reached); it rose to 80 in autumn 1975, for an overall decline of more than 80% in less than two years.

Nor is it astonishing that in these conditions competition among the various shipping lines intensified and seriously shook the cartels that had been established on some of the lines of this branch. (These cartels are known as 'conferences'.) The emergence of a new and formidable competitor, namely the Soviet merchant fleet, which is expanding headlong[8] (and secondarily the Polish and East German fleets), further accentuated this trend.

For their part, the airlines have suffered mounting financial deficits, in spite of the sustained expansion of passenger and freight traffic. These deficits led to a complete breakup of the IATA cartel, with the outbreak of a particularly intense price war over the North Atlantic route. They also led to a shrinkage of the market for civilian aeronautic construction. It is true that there are still orders for military aircraft, but they are the object of increasingly intense international competition, as is illustrated by the battle over the 'deal of the century' (the replacement of the Belgian, Dutch, and Danish Starfighters). Nevertheless, the American aerospace industry seems to have averted the recession through a 4% increase in state orders in 1974 and 1975.

---

[8] The European shipping companies are trying to defend themselves against this Soviet competition by applying protectionist measures and by luring the specialized Soviet companies into certain maritime routes within the 'conferences', i.e. the cartels that share out traffic on these routes. (For the Far East, see *Far Eastern Economic Review*, 21 December 1977; for the Atlantic, Mediterranean, and East African routes see *Business Week*, 12 December 1977.)

A typical example of a branch that had been marked by virtually uninterrupted expansion during the two preceding decades, the *electronics industry* seems to have entered a phase of mounting economic difficulties since the 1974–75 recession. A situation of pronounced excess capacity prevails in transistors and semi-conductors in general; as of mid-1975, this industry was working at only 50% capacity in the United States. The sales decline during that year was of the order of 15%.

In the domain of electronic calculators, excess capacity provoked a price collapse for pocket and small table apparatuses. There were price reductions even in the realm of computers proper. The penetration of the electronics trusts into telecommunications through the launching of *private satellites* may open important new outlets.

The Japanese electronics industry, which specializes in consumer goods like television sets and small calculators, suffered a recession in 1974, followed by a new reduction in production in 1975. In spite of the spectacular success of Japanese exports in 1976 and 1977, signs of long-term saturation are also beginning to appear in this sector. When pocket calculators were first introduced, Japan had the lion's share of the market. In 1973 it produced 10 million calculators, as against 7 million for the United States and Canada combined. In 1974 Japanese production rose to 15.5 million units, as against 12 million for the United States. But American production exceeded Japanese in 1976. The Japanese share of the European market declined from 80% in 1971–72 to 50% in 1975.

In the long run, however, these saturation phenomena affect only electronic consumer goods (including pocket calculators). In the domain of electronic capital goods, the long-term trend remains one of expansion; the computer sector continues to anticipate an annual expansion of demand of about 10% in value and 14% in volume up through 1988. This may prove to be exaggerated, but the trend towards expansion is clear.

The *machine construction industry* is probably the only key sector for which a long-term boom seems assured, primarily because of increased orders from the semi-colonial and dependent countries and the bureaucratized workers' states. These orders are expected to compensate fully for the long-term decline in investment in the imperialist countries themselves. While this prospect is generally accepted by experts, it must nevertheless be weighed against the general growth rate of the international capitalist economy anticipated in the years ahead.

It is clear that if this growth long remains largely inferior to the rates registered during the fifties and sixties – and we are convinced that it will – then instances of excess capacity will coincide in a large number of industrial branches. They will thus entail a more than proportional decline in productive investment and orders for capital goods. At the same time, modernization and rationalization investment will undoubtedly continue under these conditions. There will thus be high orders for capital goods from the OPEC countries and the most industrialized of the dependent countries. On a world scale, then, there will be a faster elimination of those enterprises working with outmoded technology and a redistribution of productive resources within the machine construction industry itself, to the advantage of companies producing highly advanced equipment (electro-nuclear installations, electronics, automatic machine-tools run by magnetic tapes, etc.), and at the expense of the sectors producing the more classical equipment (classical electrical equipment, textile machinery, etc.).

Precise figures are available for the sub-sector of machine-tools. In 1974 the major exporting, importing, and producing countries stood as shown in Table 18.

3. Monetary Pump-Priming and the Limited Duration of the Recession

Surprised by the scope of the recession, the leaders of the richest imperialist countries – primarily the United States, West Germany, and Japan – decided during the second half of 1975 to take monetary pump-priming measures, i.e. to eliminate the toughest measures of credit restriction and slowdown in the growth of the money supply that had been taken during 1974–75 in the framework of the 'struggle against inflation'. The

Table 18

Exports, Imports, and Production of Machine Tools in 1974
(in millions of current dollars)

Production		Export	
1. West Germany	2,762	1. West Germany	1,980
2. United States	2,100	2. United States	480
3. USSR	1,824	3. Switzerland	393
4. Japan	1,533	4. East Germany	392
5. Italy	756	5. Italy	303
6. France	592	6. Britain	251
7. Britain	538	7. France	251
8. East Germany	513	8. Japan	230
9. Switzerland	484	9. Czechoslovakia	180
10. Poland	337.	10. USSR	145

Import

1. USSR	368
2. France	310
3. Poland	307
4. United States	258
5. West Germany	230
6. Italy	234
7. Britain	228
8. Japan	149
9. East Germany	100
10. Czechoslovakia	100

(The absence of Brazil and the People's Republic of China from the import list seems unjustified.)

Source: *The American Machinist*, reproduced in *Le Monde*, 22 April 1975.

economic recovery in the United States was prepared by a colossal budget deficit, of the order of $70–80 thousand million for the fiscal year July 1975 to June 1976. The budget deficit in West Germany was of the order of $30 thousand million; in Japan it was of the order of $20 thousand million. If we add the considerable deficits of the public sector (state budget plus nationalized sector) in three other imperialist countries – Britain ($20 thousand million), France ($10 thousand million), and Italy ($25 thousand million) – we arrive at a figure of no less than $175 thousand million in additional purchasing power injected into the economic circuit between the middle of 1975 and the middle of 1976, solely through the budget deficits of the major imperialist countries. This figure exceeds that of the combined budget deficits of the major imperialist powers during any single year of the Second World War. It is beyond comparison with the modest 'Keynesian' experiments of the Roosevelt New Deal.

I had been willing to predict that in spite of all the noise about the 'absolute priority of the struggle against inflation', the imperialist governments would have no choice but to resort to *massive doses of Keynesian and neo-Keynesian recovery techniques* the moment a serious recession broke out simultaneously in all the major imperialist countries. In spite of appearances, and under the cover of solemn sermons in favour of 'monetary rigour', this is precisely what happened as soon as the recession assumed threatening scope.[9]

Because of the enormous injection of additional purchasing power into the economic circuit, the recession was effectively halted after about a year or a year and a half. After this a recovery began.

This confirms the correctness of a diagnosis I formulated in 1960. The bourgeois state absolutely does not command the means by which to avert economic fluctuations and the periodic new over-production crises. This is inherent in the capitalist mode of production and will disappear only when that mode of production disappears. But it does command the means by which *to limit the immediate duration and depth of the recession* through the application of Keynesian and neo-Keynesian techniques – that is, through creating false money. The price paid for the application of this anti-crisis technique is the progressive devaluation of paper money and the acceleration of inflation. The limit of the application of the anti-crisis techniques is reached when inflation, having exhausted the bulk of

[9] *Le Monde* (6 December 1977) published an article by Professor A. Cotta suggestively entitled 'Nous sommes tous keynésiens' ('We are all Keynesians'), in which he correctly affirmed: 'In spite of the frenetic agitation of the monetarists, there is no western country in which the growth of the money supply does not already exceed that of real national product or in which the real interest rate (the nominal rate adjusted to eliminate inflation) has not become virtually nil.'

the reserves of an imperialist power, begins to run rampant, loses any effect of stimulating economic activity, and even provokes negative effects.

An attentive study of the successive recessions since the Second World War permits the effects and limits of the anti-crisis techniques to be indicated clearly. They can prevent neither the outbreak of crises nor their initial gravity. But they can muffle their effects over time, i.e. they can prevent their cumulative development into a 'snowball effect'. A comparison between the economic fluctuations of the first nine months of the 1957–58 recession and of the 1929–32 economic crisis in the United States is particularly instructive in this regard, even though the 1957–58 recession lasted only a year while the 1929–32 crisis lasted three and a half years. The basic figures are indicated in Table 19.

Table 19

*Economic Changes During the First Nine Months of Crisis
in the United States (in %)*[10]

	1929–32	1957–58
Employment (non-agricultural)	− 6.5	− 4.2
GNP	− 5.5	− 4.1
Industrial Production	−15.9	−13.1
Volume of retail sales	− 6.1	− 5.1
Orders for durable goods	−26.5	−20.1

But the tendency of inflation to accelerate more and more during the year prior to the 1974–75 recession had three consequences. In all the imperialist countries, *greater and greater* sums of money must be injected into the circuit in order to halt the recession and generate a 'recovery', even a modest one. The weakest imperialist countries – particularly those suffering from a higher than average inflation rate – proved incapable of effecting such an increase in the money supply, for to do so would have entailed state bankruptcy and have paralysed economic activity. Even the rich countries had to moderate the application of the anti-crisis techniques so as to avert runaway

[10] E. Mandel, *Marxist Economic Theory*, op. cit., Vol. II, p. 532.

inflation, which immediately reduced the efficacy of the recovery measures.

Thus, the growth of the money supply in the United States remained confined to limits of about 5–7% a year in 1976 and 6.5–7% in 1977, these limits being set by the conservative Arthur Burns, then chairman of the Federal Reserve Board (not so conservative when it comes to the scope of the budget deficit, however). The advocates of 'unbridled' neo-Keynesian recovery techniques wanted a 9–10% annual increase in the money supply, which would probably have implied a yearly budget deficit exceeding $100 thousand million.

One of the reasons for the refusal to take the much more extensive recovery measures that would have been required to neutralize the effects of a recession as serious as that of 1974–75 was undoubtedly fear of stimulating inflation, which was already approaching a dangerous threshold in most of the imperialist countries ('double digit inflation') and had to some extent exceeded that level in Britain, Italy, and France. It has thus been confirmed again that late capitalism is incapable of escaping this dilemma: either aggravated recession or accentuated inflation. Moreover, in the long run, runaway inflation itself eventually provokes increasingly serious economic crises.

A second reason for the refusal to take more sweeping recovery measures is related to the incidence of inter-imperialist competition. Granted, so long as the system of floating exchange rates is maintained, the aggravation of domestic inflation no longer automatically entails a deterioration of a country's competitive position, since the increased costs on the domestic market are in large part neutralized as far as export prices are concerned by the fall in the exchange rate of the currency involved. Under these conditions, accelerated inflation can even have the effect of improving the competitive position of the country suffering the disease – at least in the short run. Indeed, this is one of the reasons why some of the imperialist powers consider the system of floating exchange rates to be a means of disloyal competition that ought to be proscribed.

Nevertheless, an inflation rate in one country considerably higher than the prevailing rate in competitor countries still entails unfavourable economic consequences for that country in the long run. When domestic demand is inflated, imports rise as well; in addition, they automatically increase in value as a very result of the decline in the exchange rate of the national currency, which protects exports from the effects of inflation. Hence, despite the system of floating exchange rates, inflation continues to worsen the balance of payments deficit and therefore increases dependence on international credit; it thus weakens the overall competitive position of the imperialist power in question. In addition, more and more commodities must be exported (which means more quantities of labour) in order to purchase the same volume of foreign commodities. The nation is thus impoverished, gradually losing a portion of national economic wealth.

The strategy of pursuing inter-imperialist competition through the weapon of an inflation rate higher than that of competitors thus leads to a sharp reduction in domestic consumption, i.e. to a radical modification of the division of the national income at the expense of the workers and to the advantage of capitalist profits. The relationship of socio-political forces, however, does not yet permit the radical application of such a strategy by any imperialist country. Hence the relative moderation of the recovery measures, except in the United States, where the rate of inflation was brought down in spite of the enormous budget deficit, primarily because of the enormous reserves of the U.S. economy and precisely because of the relative weakness of the workers' movement and the reactions of the workers.

Those responsible for economic policy in the imperialist countries, as well as many economists, continue to claim that the measures of monetary and credit expansion automatically entail a more than proportional upturn in industrial production, as a result of the famous multiplier factor. They also count on the so-called technical effects of the automatic growth of inventories, once these have reached too low a level. After the phase of 'inventory liquidation' at the beginning of the crisis, merchants and industrialists must necessarily increase inventories again, even to maintain a level of activity inferior to that of the previous phase of prosperity. This entails a rise in orders, and therefore in employment, incomes, and consumption, which leads to a new rise in production and employment, and so on. Now, during the first quarter of 1975 inventories in the United States diminished at an annual rate of $18 thousand million, although they had risen at the same rate during the preceding quarter. The new turn in the cycle, then, could not have been far off, according to this view.

All this neo-Keynesian reasoning contains many unwarranted generalizations, if not pure and simple errors in logic and analysis, founded primarily on the manipulation of undifferentiated aggregates. I have already highlighted these abuses on various occasions.[11] The only certain conclusion is that a vigorous stimulation of demand through an accelerated expansion of the money supply *will surely halt the fall in demand for consumer goods.* When the government distributes tens of thousands of millions of additional dollars to consumers, the volume of current sales of consumer goods can hardly decline. The fact that unemployment compensation reaches rather high levels nowadays, contrary to the thirties (this compensation varies from 44% to 80% of wages and can sometimes even exceed wages because of the effects of the decline in taxes in certain limited cases), contributes to limiting the decline in demand for consumer goods already resulting from the recession.

Any other conclusion, however, remains to be demonstrated. It is not certain that sales will rise *in the same proportion* as the incomes of consumers, primarily because fear of unemployment can induce a portion of the working class and the petty bourgeoisie to increase their savings so as to guard against an anticipated reduction in current income in the future. Indeed, the Shadow Open Market Committee in the United States estimates that household savings rose from $76.7 thousand million in 1974 to $80 thousand million in 1975.

[11] A good critique of Keynesian illusions may be found in Rudolf Hickel, op. cit., as well as André Gunder Frank, 'The Economist as Soothsayer and Ideologist: The Clouded Ball and Keynesian Class Policy', a chapter in a forthcoming book on the economic crisis.

Moreover, the practice of hire purchase and the rather high debt of consumer households likewise entail a reduction in *current* consumption expenditures when incomes decline. Recourse to new consumer credit for the purchase of durable consumer goods also declines in time of crisis. Paradoxically, one may thus expect an increase in the rate of savings during periods of recession.[12] Thus, a portion of the increased money supply may simply swell bank deposits or reduce the rate of circulation of money, without augmenting the volume of sales of commodities and thus without stimulating an upturn in production.

Furthermore, the swelling of the money supply and the various subsidies distributed to capitalist companies in no way entail any automatic upturn in productive investment. In order for the capitalists to utilize the credit facilities placed at their disposal, they must anticipate both a rise in the rate of profit and an expansion of the market. They do not increase production simply because it becomes easier for them to do so. They increase production only to maintain or increase their profits. This presupposes that the increased production can be sold, and under profitable conditions that enable the capitalists to reverse the fall in profits that had caused the crisis and was aggravated at the beginning of the recession.

Now, the re-establishment of the rate of profit is scarcely automatic during a recession. Thus, in spite of the increased credit facilities, the lowering of the discount rate and of

[12] 'Unexpected increases of the household saving ratio . . . seem to have strongly contributed to the deepness of the latest international recession and to the underestimation of recessionary forces by economic forecasters and policy makers' (Franz Ettlin, 'Swedish Private Consumption and Saving During Two Decades', in Skandinavska Enskilda Banken *Quarterly Review*, 3–4, 1976). The December 1975 study of the OECD cited above assumes a *long-term* trend of growth in the savings rate because of the increase in nominal incomes. This appears doubtful to us, since inflation persists. In *Les perspectives économiques de l'OCDE* (no. 21, July 1977, p. 29) it is pointed out that on the contrary this rate of increase is tending to decline in countries like the United States and France. In the United States the household savings rate for 1977 fell back to its 1963 level. In France it is now at the 1968 level. For West Germany the 1977–78 *Jahresgutachten* of the Sachverständigenrat registers an increase in the household savings rate between 1967 and 1974, followed by a steep decline which takes it back to the late 1969 level by the end of 1977.

interest rates in general, and the increase in the money supply, it is perfectly possible for the volume of credit to companies to continue to diminish, not because the supply of money-capital is diminishing, but because the demand for this money-capital on the part of entrepreneurs is lacking. Indeed, on 7 May 1975 the total volume of bank credit to American companies stood at $128.6 thousand million, lower than at the beginning of April ($129.4 thousand million), the beginning of March ($129.7 thousand million), the beginning of February ($129.6 thousand million), and the beginning of January ($132.8 thousand million), in spite of all the recovery measures that had already been taken.

Finally, one must take account of the incidence of the contraction of exports, which can neutralize the effects of a modest recovery of sales on the domestic market, especially in countries that export a relatively high fraction of their industrial production. Under these conditions, the moment of recovery is retarded until the *combined effect* of the recovery of domestic demand in all the major imperialist countries enables the contraction of world trade to be halted.

4. The Fear of a Bank Panic

There is an additional reason why the bourgeoisie hesitated to accept the doses of inflation that are now necessary to stimulate a stronger upturn: they would have entailed mounting risks of upsetting the entire credit system and even of triggering an outright generalized bank panic. Any over-production crisis inevitably implies a considerable rise in the number of bankruptcies and collapses of firms. Although the small and middle-sized companies are hit harder than the powerful trusts, the more serious the recession, the greater will be the number of large trusts that will also be drawn into the maelstrom. Indeed, the objective function of the crisis is precisely to eliminate the 'dead wood', the less profitable companies, be they great or small.

Now, in a climate of protracted inflation and growing indebtedness of all capitalist firms, what is impossible for the 'little man' – namely to amass greater wealth by going into debt (borrowing 'good money' and repaying loans with devalued money ten years later) – becomes quite possible for the 'big fish', whose power and influence in the state are supposed to protect them should anything go wrong.[13] The profit-earning capacity of many of the great corporations thus becomes increasingly enigmatic. Bank analysts have greater and greater difficulty getting at the truth behind the elaborate account sheets.

Inflation feeds the relative abundance of money-capital which the banks are able to provide. The scope of banking operations thus expands at an accelerated rate. The competence of top bank officials, who are supposed to decide whether to grant credit and to evaluate whether firms are sound, inevitably declines as recruitment speeds up. The atmosphere of sharpened competition prevailing among the banks frequently impels them to take greater risks, especially since their faith in expansion and uninterrupted inflation makes those risks appear smaller.

In 1974 the publication of *The Bankers* by Martin Mayer, a conservative expert, made a big impression on the American bourgeoisie. In his book Mayer described the various new techniques responsible for the rise of more 'aggressive' bank practices since the beginning of the sixties. These practices were notably reflected in the banking heresy of massively employing short-term deposits to finance long-term loans and in an increasingly rapid expansion of the total volume of credit relative to the funds of the banks themselves. (Moreover, a

---

[13] This applies not only to the imperialist countries, but also to the most industrialized dependent countries. See the highly elegant description of the slump of the Brazilian textile industry in the *Gazeta Mercantil* of Sao Paulo (English-language edition of July 1977): 'During the first six months, thousands of small and medium-sized textile firms encountered difficulties in financing their working capital. Those that managed it in private banks paid from 50% to 60% annual interest, thus transferring much of their profits to the banks. While the majority of firms faced this kind of problem, the government, through the National Economic Development Bank, made available more than Cr. 500 million [$40 million] to "save" a bankrupt company, the S/A Fiaçao e Tecelagem Lutfalla.'

considerable portion of this credit was of doubtful recoverability or of a speculative nature.)

Of course, the solvency of American private banks ultimately depends on the behaviour of the Federal Reserve System, the American central bank. To all appearances, the big bourgeoisie was convinced that the central bank would intervene to rescue any big bank facing closure, no matter what the cost to the economy as a whole.

Mayer correctly emphasized the real dilemma facing the central bank: it cannot refuse so much credit to the banks as to *compel* them to clean up their own credit system, for such a refusal would indeed threaten to provoke the collapse of several big banks, and this could touch off a chain reaction leading to a genuine bank panic. Nevertheless, without this sort of severe pressure, the private banks threaten not to correct their adventurist policy. Mayer concluded: 'There are billions of dollars in potentially lost loans in the system; we are coming closer and closer to an explosion. The present banking structure *can* collapse. And the more the regulatory apparatus allows it to grow, the more catastrophic the collapse will be.'[14]

There are some signs that the American banking system is now returning to more orthodox practices. But the root of the problem remains. What is involved here is not so much a question of the variations in the individual psychology of bankers, some being more 'adventurist', others more 'conservative'. Rather, it is a question of the general consequence of the atmosphere of inflation, speculation, and fiscal evasion and fraud; to this must be added the growing interrelations among the banks, the 'business world', political lobbies, state purchases, and the corruption of functionaries, politicians, and businessmen. All this eventually leads to corruption of bankers, who are supposed to stand above suspicion.[15]

[14] Martin Mayer, *The Bankers*, New York, 1974.

[15] An amusing parody, obviously exaggerated but only partially imaginary, of this imbrication of 'high finance and the underworld' is provided by the three novels of Paul Erdman – *The Billion Dollar Killing, The Silver Bears,* and *The Crash of '79* – which deal with speculation in gold, silver, and petrodollars respectively. Erdman himself comes from financial circles and did time in prison for financial fraud.

The number of bankruptcies in the United States rose more than 30% during the 1974–75 recession, in Britain more than 60%. There were 7,500 bankruptcies in West Germany in 1974 and 8,600 in Japan in 1975 (14,000 in 1977). On the eve and at the beginning of the recession a wave of bankruptcies swept banks and financial corporations: the Herstadt Bank of Cologne; the Franklin Bank, the National Bank of San Diego, and the Italian Sindona group, which dominated them. Some 'secondary banks' and several British financial groups also collapsed, as did the International Credit Bank (an Israeli bank established in Switzerland).

Many finance companies in the City of London specializing in real-estate speculation were dragged into the vortex, notably the Lyon group, the Jessel insurance company, London & County Securities, and the Triumph Investment Trust. According to *The Economist*: 'The collapse in the property market posed a bigger threat to Britain's financial system than the withdrawal of deposits from secondary banks. On realistic property evaluations, a number of banks are insolvent in all but name. . . . By the end of 1974, bank lending to the property and construction industries had reached £5 billion. That's more than half the banks' commitment to all of British manufacturing, although the ratio had been a little more than one-fifth in 1970. . . . How much property is overhanging the market? Over £1 billion at 1973 values, including the portfolios of the private Stern and Lyon groups, and the quoted Guardian Properties (Holdings), which collapsed last year, is probably in the hands of receivers and liquidators.'[16]

Once again, there is nothing fortuitous about these successive bankruptcies. The 1972–73 boom had been essentially speculative. Speculation in real estate – and raw materials – is an inevitable by-product of accelerated inflation. The more productive investment slackens or stagnates, the more the banks, which possess an abundance of liquidity, are compelled to seek lucrative investments elsewhere, including real estate deals. The crisis of the construction industry, along with that of the

[16] *The Economist*, 9 August 1975.

automobile industry, detonated the 1974–75 recession and inevitably provoked a collapse in the prices of construction sites; hence the insolvency of many companies specializing in real-estate financing. These serial bankruptcies were brought about by a genuine internal logic of the system.

The British secondary banks experienced very severe difficulties. Twenty-six of them were saved only by considerable support from the major banks. Among these were United Dominion Trust, the largest private finance company in Britain, the First National Finance Corporation, which went into banking deals at the beginning of the seventies, and Sterling Industrial Securities. Even the venerable and mysterious Crown Agents, which is said to manage the London holdings of ninety governments throughout the world, lost no less than £212 million in imprudent commitments to secondary banks and companies financing real-estate speculation. The Crown Agents was saved from bankruptcy only by a gift of £85 million from the British government, and by a state guarantee of all its deposits. A similar case was the spectacular bankruptcy of the Spanish Sofico group (caused by a combination of the sharp decline in international tourism brought on by the recession and real-estate speculation).

The repercussions of real-estate speculation on the banking system were quantitatively more severe in the United States than in Britain, although the consequences were less grave, because of the greater reserves of the American banking system. Between 1969 and 1971, when real estate investment trusts (REIT) were in vogue, these companies sold some $6 thousand million worth of shares. During the recession these shares lost 70% of their value. Even the real estate investment trust linked to a bank as powerful as Chase Manhattan (the Chase Manhattan Real Estate Investment Trust) suffered a decline in share value falling from $70 to $4. The big New York banks are now holding a total of $7 thousand million in nonguaranteed real-estate loans and $4 thousand million in REIT shares whose value is less than certain.

Moreover, these are not at all the only dubious loans and assets held by these big banks. When the sudden threat that the

City of New York might go bankrupt loomed on the horizon in autumn 1975[17] it was reported that at the time the twelve largest New York banks were holding more than $4 thousand million in 'bad debts' ($2 thousand million in obligations of the City of New York, $1 thousand million in loans to airline companies, $400 million in loans to W. T. Grant, and more than $500 million in loans to other municipal governments threatened by bankruptcy).[18] And all this comes on top of the $11 thousand million in doubtful real-estate loans.

In certain cases the total of the bank's capital and its reserves with which to cover losses on defaulted loans was less than the total value of the REITs and the obligations of the nearly bankrupt City of New York. As of 1975 this was the case for at least two of the twelve largest New York banks, Chemical and Banker's Trust. The Maritime Midlands Bank, also one of the 'big twelve', had already registered losses for the fourth quarter of 1975. The Federal Reserve System has committed itself to prop up the big banks come what may. To this end, however, it keeps close watch on no fewer than 546 banks whose fate is cause for concern.[19]

The Bank of England accorded a similar guarantee to five big British banks in order to cover the salvage operation for the secondary banks and finance companies. It is reported to have 'covered' or guaranteed inter-bank loans totalling $3 thousand million, notably £70 million to prop up Slater Walker Securities (a speculative outfit put together by Peter Walker, later a

[17] On this threat see in particular *The Economist*, 18 and 25 October 1975.

[18] The bankruptcy of W. T. Grant & Co., one of the largest U.S. commercial companies, cost the banking system dearly. A total of $640 million had been loaned to W. T. Grant. The company's debts to three major New York banks – Chase Manhattan, First National City, and Morgan Guarantee Trust – amounted to nearly $100 million each.

[19] The situation of American banks improved somewhat in 1976. Nevertheless, in its 22 November 1976 issue the magazine *U.S. News and World Report* noted: 'According to a report of the Federal Deposit Insurance Corporation, eight American banks with more than a billion dollars in deposits are encountering some difficulty; one of them is in "serious difficulty".' For the first three-quarters of 1977 the Marine Midland Bank registered only a modest profit of $11 million. The story has a sensational ending: in early 1978 the Marine Midland Bank, one of the largest in the United States, was absorbed by the British-owned Hong Kong and Shanghai Corporation.

Minister in the Conservative government of Edward Heath, and Jim Slater, who was considered to be a financial 'wizard' during the sixties and early seventies) and another £70 million to the private London bank of Edward Bates, 25% of whose assets are held by Arab capital.

Some of the most important banks of the capitalist world, such as Chase Manhattan, Union des Banques Suisses, the Lugano branch of Lloyd's of London, the Banque de Bruxelles, the Westdeutsche Landesbank, and the Hessische Landesbank (Helaba) suffered significant losses in *currency speculation*, although these losses did not endanger their liquidity. Total losses for the first five of these banks have been estimated at $300 million. The total losses of Helaba during the recession are said to be on the order of $1 thousand million. Some private French banks also had difficulties, but they came through thanks to aid from the big nationalized deposit banks.

In the case of Helaba, the exchange losses were compounded by the bank's shares in the bankrupt Banque de Crédit International established in Geneva by the Israeli financier Rosenbaum and in the 'Manhattan Centre', a Brussels shopping mall and office complex which went bankrupt. The Westdeutsche Landesbank, Germany's third largest bank, was led by Poullain, its director, into an attempt to salvage the Württembergische Kreditverein (total deposits of $1.5 thousand million), which was on the brink of bankruptcy. More than $100 million in loans were accorded through an intermediary. This affair was one of the reasons for the ouster of Poullain at the end of 1977.[20]

All signs are that the increasingly intense internationalization of production and capital heightens the risk of the outbreak of chain reactions once a few spectacular bankruptcies occur. If a large number of bourgeois and petty-bourgeois bank customers stampede to the windows to withdraw their deposits simultaneously – that is, if a real bank panic erupts – the entire credit system could be paralysed.

Now, credit plays a much more important role in the economy of the imperialist countries today than it did in 1929. Such

[20] *Der Spiegel*, 2 January 1978.

paralysis would thus precipitate a crisis even more severe than that of 1929. The international bourgeoisie is fully aware of this. The spectre of just such a panic emerged after the crash of the Herstadt Bank and the Sindona group, the financial crisis of the City of New York, and the difficulties of Continental Mortgage Investors, an American real-estate finance company that was unable to repay a loan of 80 million Euro-dollars that had been accorded by a consortium of European banks. The presidents of the central banks of the major imperialist countries met in Basle and, with the support of the leaders of the big deposit banks, decided that they would not permit the collapse of any bank of any importance in any imperialist country. They then made this decision known to the international bourgeois public. The payment difficulties of Continental Mortgage Investors were eliminated by an immediate intervention by European and American financiers, who accorded this company a new loan of $150 million.[21] The immediate fears were therefore assuaged. Once again, the banking system was battered but not knocked out. Reserves are still far from exhausted. The infernal cycle of 'debt-inflation-aggravated debt-threat to the solvency of the banking system' continues to lurk in the background. For the moment, however, it is merely lurking.[22]

It is clear, however, that there are objective limits to the banking system's capacity for self-correction – if galloping

[21] On the relationships among cyclical crises, bank competition, capital flight, and 'unorthodox' banking practices, see the Crédit Suisse affair, treated in Chapter Four.

[22] An additional threat of collapse of the international credit system results from the uncontrollable expansion of the market in Euro-currencies. Here is the view of M. Rennie, an international banker highly esteemed in financial circles: 'The overall power of the international monetary system is too dependent on reasonable stability in each sector to allow such a major collapse to occur (in Euro-markets) without every effort being made, internationally, to avert it. . . . Should a very important bankruptcy occur despite a maximum of international cooperation, it could, in my opinion, undermine the viability of Euromarkets and oust them from their position in today's world financial scene' (*The Banker*, August 1975). It was to avert such a collapse that the meeting of the governors of the central banks of eight major European imperialist countries, held in Basle in July 1974, decided to act as 'last ditch lender' for private banks in difficulty. In October 1974 the United States and Japan joined

inflation is to be averted. What will happen if insolvency strikes not just one medium-sized bank but several major banks, if the hole to be plugged is not one of several hundred million dollars but $10 thousand million.[23] In Britain the 'big five' grimaced when they had to lay out the $250 million needed to salvage the secondary banks.[24] Would the banking system survive a $10 thousand million test? Will that test come during the next recession? That is a mystery that no economist, government minister, or director of any monopolist industrial trust can illuminate. Such is the cloud that continues to hang over the entire operation of 'economic recovery'. It is a good-sized cloud, commensurate with the very scope of inflation, and it can only grow as inflation itself rises.

The governments in the imperialist countries have sought to toughen banking legislation and regulations so as to reduce the risks of serious accidents and prevent banking capital from plunging into too many imprudent operations. Any genuine public control of the private banks, however, faces two difficulties. First, it conflicts with the logic of private property, competition, and the effort to maximize profits, all of which imply major risks which the controllers can register only after the fact (if the dice come up wrong). Second, a really severe set

---

this agreement. Nevertheless, the accord does not detail exactly how the possible losses accrued by these salvage operations would be shared. (See 'International Debt, the Banks, and U.S. Foreign Policy', a staff report prepared for the use of the Subcommittee on Foreign Economic Policy of the Committee on Foreign Relations of the U.S. Senate, U.S. Government Printing Office, Washington, 1977, p. 26.)

[23] 'Two great problems nearly halted operations in Eurocurrencies in the middle of 1974. The initial practice of the oil exporting countries was to place their surpluses as very short-term deposits solely in well-established big banks, especially in the United States and Switzerland. By itself, this probably would not have upset the system. But the bankruptcy of some banks shook confidence in the inter-banking market, and many small banks even had difficulty completing their existing operations. The atmosphere improved after the governors of the central banks of the Group of Ten issued an assurance in September 1974 that they would come to the aid of international banks in difficulty. . . . The overall result was that a relatively limited number of big world banks became, for the moment at least, a dominant force without real rival in the system' (P. A. Wellens, 'Les emprunts des pays en développement sur le marché des Euro-dollars', OECD, Paris, 1977, p. 25).

[24] *The Times*, 13 December 1974.

of regulations would be effective only if it entailed penalization (for example, a cutoff of central bank credits to banks that violate the regulations); but that would have *contrary* effects, for it would touch off precisely the sort of chain reaction that would lead to the panic that any such regulations would have been designed to avert.[25]

[25] A good analysis of these contradictions – even though it is purely technical – is provided by Daniel Deguen and Jacques-Henri David: 'Les mesures prises pour renforcer les garanties de liquidité et de solvabilité financières', published in the magazine *Banque*, October 1976.

3

Uneven Recovery and Inter-imperialist Contradictions

1. Fundamental Causes of the Recession

Precisely because the 'anti-crisis' practices of governments once again succeeded in limiting the duration and depth of the recession, although less so than in the past; and precisely because the bourgeois state did refloat many banks, finance companies, and major trusts that found themselves on the brink of bankruptcy, the recession did not play the traditional objective role of capitalist crises: 'to prune the capitalist economy'. That is why the recession of 1974–75 was not followed by a new boom.

The generalized recession of 1974–75 was the product neither of bad luck nor of some sort of 'freak accident' of the international capitalist economy (such as the rise in oil prices). It resulted from all the basic contradictions of the capitalist mode of production, which rose to the surface after being partially contained by the inflation of two decades of accelerated growth (two and a half decades in the United States).

To determine whether the recession will be followed by a new protracted phase of accelerated growth or whether, on the contrary, it signals the reversal of the long-term economic trend, one must examine the recession's repercussions on the *major factors that influence the long-term evolution of the rate of profit in the imperialist countries.*

(1) A new decline in the prices of raw materials seems extremely improbable in coming years. Particularly as far as the cost of energy is concerned, imperialist capital (with the possible exception of capital in Japan and some minor coun-

tries) and the bourgeoisies of the semi-colonial and dependent countries have a common interest in preventing the price of the oil exported by the OPEC countries *from falling below a certain threshold.* Any 'excessive' decline in this price would render uncompetitive alternative energy sources in which immense investments have been made (North Sea and Alaskan oil, shale oil and bituminous sands in the United States, nuclear energy, and soon, probably, solar energy). Even if the decline in the price scales of raw materials continues during the phases of recovery, which is also improbable, these prices will not return to the pre-1972–73 boom levels.[1]

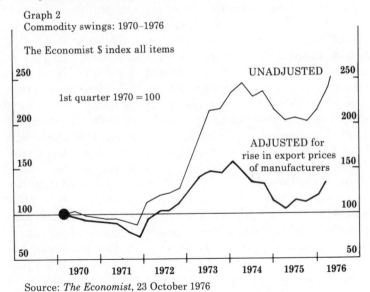

Graph 2
Commodity swings: 1970–1976

The Economist $ index all items

Source: *The Economist*, 23 October 1976

(2) The effects of the third technological revolution on the reduction of the value of the elements of fixed capital – despite

---

[1] Anthony Sampson's *The Seven Sisters*, London, 1976, gives a detailed description of the complex relations among the long-term price (and profit) strategies of the giant oil companies, the functioning of OPEC, and its decision to quadruple oil prices in October 1973. The mutual dependence – and collaboration – between the private cartel of the companies and the public cartel of OPEC is well illustrated.

the extension of semi-automation, the organic composition of capital rose less rapidly during the period 1940 (or 1948) to 1968 than could have been supposed at first sight – seem to be slackening in the long run. Indeed, the rate of increase in the productivity of labour will decline somewhat in both Department I and Department II, which will entail at once a gradual rise in the cost of the total mass of machinery utilized by industrial capital and a slowdown in the growth of relative surplus-value (the growth of which had been another of the striking features of the third technological revolution). It is true that for computers proper the fall in value will not really begin to become apparent, belatedly, until the subsequent phase, that of the fourth generation.

(3) The 1974–75 recession did not cause a massive devalorization of capital, the precondition for permitting a serious recovery of the rate of profit. Granted there was, as we have already noted, a considerable rise in the number of bankruptcies. Nonetheless, the immense majority of enterprises affected were small and medium-sized ones. Major industrial and commercial bankruptcies, apart from those already cited, were limited to a few cases: the W. T. Grant Company in the United States (greatest bankruptcy in the country since the collapse of the Penn Central Railroad, with more than a 1000 million dollars in debts); the Japanese textile trust Kohjin ($500 million in debts); the Japanese Sakamoto Spinning Company ($213 million in debt); the Japanese finance group Ataka (nearly $900 million in debts); the Japanese wood industry and prefabricated housing construction company Eidai, whose debacle was the worst in Japanese capitalist history: $1 thousand million in bad debts. There were also the difficulties of the Hutchinson International group in Hong Kong.

The fact that so few great monopolies collapsed during such a severe recession is not at all the result of the allegedly solid financial situation of most of them. On the contrary, some, and not the least important – we need only mention Chrysler, whose profits were only 1.5% of turnover in 1977, coming on top of severe losses during the recession, or Lockheed, whose future does not look bright – came close to catastrophe on several occasions. No, the reason for the survival of the least profitable monopolies lies in the fact that the banking system continues to accord them credit, that the central banks and the bourgeois state continue to bail them out. 'If we were not living in a country so respectful of open secrets when it comes to business,' wrote French financial journalist Paul Fabre, 'it would long since have been reported in the press that Rhône-Poulenc [the major French chemicals monopoly] would have had difficulty meeting its obligations had it not been for the banking credit that continues to be accorded it.'[2] The case of Kohjin is particularly eloquent: business is continuing as though nothing was wrong. Enormous credit was accorded a company that was in reality bankrupt.

As for the European automobile trusts, some of which were in extreme difficulties, there was the no less peremptory statement by the French minister Gobert: 'In fact, a state guarantee has already been explicitly accorded all the great European automobile companies. Governments cannot abandon them.' In addition, state subsidies of all sorts and massive fiscal injections were also granted.[3]

The consequence of state guarantees being systematically accorded to the least profitable monopolies is an increasingly pronounced debt, and this clearly limits the rise in the average rate of profit for the great trusts. In 1968 the proportion of internal to external financing for non-financial corporations in the United States was 2 to 1: by 1975 it had fallen to 2 to 3. This means that for each dollar of non-distributed profits retained by these firms there is now three times as much in outstanding bank credit or other external obligations. Twelve years ago the total value of the shares of these companies was more than four times the total volume of their debts; today the volume of these debts ($1–300 thousand million, twice the 1965 level) already amounts to more than 50% of the total value of their shares.

---

[2] *Le Monde*, 6 November 1975. Since then Rhône-Poulenc has had to effect a drastic restructuration of its textile sector (*Le Monde*, 21 and 22 December 1977).

[3] *Business Week*, 1 September 1975. In this regard see the interesting work of Anicet Le Pors, *Les Réquilles du Capital*, Le Seuil, Paris, 1977.

Debt servicing represented only 9% of the gross receipts of American companies in 1959; by 1975 it represented 33%.

In France medium- and long-term company debt rose from 30 thousand million francs in 1972 to 37 thousand million in 1973 to 44 thousand million in 1974 to 62.6 thousand million in 1975 and to 74 thousand million in 1976, according to the statistics of the national accounting service. In Italy the proportion between debts and internal financing rose from 2.2-to-1 in 1968 to 3.4-to-1 in 1972, and to 3.8-to-1 in 1976, although the volume of investment scarcely increased (statistics of the Mediobanca). A good portion of new debts serve to pay back old ones, and even to pay interest on old debts. For the nationalized companies, personnel expenses as a percentage of turnover declined from 24% in 1968 to 21.5% in 1976; during the same period the equivalent figure for financial charges rose from 6.7% to 9.6%. In Japan the relationship of debts to capital for all companies rose from 60% in 1954 to 140% in 1970.

In sum, the crisis did not cause a given mass of surplus-value to be associated with a capital heavily reduced in value. Instead there has been a redistribution of the mass of surplus-value to the advantage of the monopolies (especially the monopolies of certain branches) and at the expense of the less important companies of the middle and petty bourgeoisie. Many of these problems are obviously masked by inflation. But a profound process of 'pruning' of the system, with a sharp new rise in the rate of profit through the devalorization and massive destruction of capital, simply did not take place.

(4) One of the usual effects of any over-production crisis and massive extension of unemployment is an increase in the rate of surplus-value through mechanisms inherent in the process of production itself. This did indeed occur during and just after the 1974–75 recession. Unemployment and fear of unemployment increased 'labour discipline', reduced sick leaves (that is, impelled workers to stay at work even when they felt an illness coming on), reduced fluctuations in the work force, and facilitated speed-up and the intensification of the labour process. All these aspects of 'rationalization' clearly have beneficial effects on capitalist profits.

Profits did indeed rise again towards the end of the recession and the beginning of the recovery, as is clearly shown by the figures in Tables 20 and 21. In Belgium gross corporation profits

Table 20

Gross Company Profits Per Share in West Germany
(in thousands of millions of current DM)

Year		Growth compared to previous year
1973	20.8	—
1974	19.5	− 5.8%
1975	19.97	+ 2.2%
1976	23.2	+16.0%

Table 21

Evolution of Net Profits Per Share of the 880 Largest United States Companies

From 3rd quarter 1975 to 3rd quarter 1976	*From 1st quarter 1976 to 1st quarter 1977*	*From 3rd quarter 1976 to 3rd quarter 1977*
+30%	+11%	+13%

Source: Quarterly tables on these companies published in *Business Week.*

increased 16% in 1976 over 1975; profits for the first seven months of 1977 were 45.3% higher than profits for the corresponding period of 1976.

Nevertheless, the increase in the rate of surplus-value was not of sufficient scope to generate a considerable increase in the rate and mass of profit. The reason for this is social and political: the tenacious and sometimes fierce resistance of the working class and the workers' movement to the offensive of the employers which, as usual, accompanied the period of recession and the aggravation of unemployment.

What makes the present situation so serious for capitalism is precisely the coincidence of the generalized economic recession – followed by a hesitant recovery, i.e. a protracted period of heavily slowed growth – *and an exceptionally high level of*

*organization, numerical strength, and combativity of the prole-
tariat, combined with the exceptionally pronounced political
weakness of the bourgeois system.*

This coincidence is not fortuitous. It results from the entire
worldwide economic, social, and political evolution of the past
quarter century. For big capital the world relationship of
forces has clearly deteriorated. The long period of expansion
in the imperialist countries objectively increased the weight
and strength of the working class. The new rise of struggles in
West Europe since May 1968 has subjectively strengthened the
combativity and anti-capitalist consciousness of the workers
in many countries. Nowhere has the bourgeoisie been able to
inflict such defeats on the working class that they rendered the
workers unable to respond to a considerable decline in their
purchasing power and an aggravation of their living and
working conditions or to a radical undoing of their indirect
social benefits.

This is the fundamental difference between the present situation and that of 1929–32. Under these conditions, it is clear that
a struggle for a sharp and substantial increase in the rate of
exploitation of the working class will occur in the late seventies
and the eighties just as it did in the late twenties and the
thirties. But the working class enters this period of sharpened
class struggle with forces and weapons vastly superior to those
of fifty years ago. In all the imperialist countries, including the
United States, West Germany, and Japan, the decisive tests of
strength lie ahead of us and not behind us.

It is thus extremely unlikely that the international capitalist
economy will be able to return to the growth rates it enjoyed
during the fifties and sixties. The 'long wave of slackened
economic growth' which I predicted in 1965 became a reality as
of the late sixties. It will be with us for a long time, with all the
attendant consequences in all spheres of social life.

2. A Feeble Recovery and the Persistence of Chronic
Unemployment

The generalized recession of the international capitalist

economy ended in 1975, first in the United States, later in West Germany, Japan, and the other imperialist countries. In 1976 and 1977 the international capitalist economy was in a phase of recovery.

From a Marxist point of view, there is but one criterion by which to judge whether there is a recession or recovery in economic activity: the trend of material production and, closely linked to this, the trend of the accumulation of capital (the volume and rate of reinvestment of profits). To regard a decline in unemployment or a rise in real wages (in the real incomes of the labouring population) as decisive in determining a recovery is to misunderstand the very nature of the capitalist system. The latter is a system of production in which profit and the accumulation of capital are the aims of economic activity. The volume of employment and the evolution of real wages are merely by-products.

Indeed, the 'ideal' situation for capitalism is precisely one which permits a combination of the expansion of material production, a high level of unemployment, a stagnation of real wages (or very moderate wage increases), and a strong increase in profits and the accumulation of capital. Production and surplus-value break records precisely when such combinations

Table 22

Evolution of Industrial Production (in %)

Country	1975	1976
United States	− 8.9	+10.0
West Germany	− 6.2	+ 8.5
Japan	−10.9	+13.5
France	− 7.3	+10.0
Britain	− 4.8	+ 0.8
Italy	− 9.8	+12.5
Canada	− 4.6	+ 4.0
Australia	− 6.3	+ 5.5
Belgium	−10.0	+ 9.0
Sweden	− 1.8	− 1.0

Source: Väckens Affärer, 2 September 1976; *National Institute Economic Review*, February 1977; GATT, *Le Commerce international 1976/77.*

occur. Such a coincidence has not occurred during every period of recovery in the history of industrial capitalism over the past 150 years. Nor was it perfectly realized in 1976–77. It was, however, approached. In any event, this is certainly no reason to contest the fact that the economic cycle turned up in 1976 and 1977.

The reversal of the cycle is clearly expressed in the figures in Table 22.

But while the recovery is real, it is relatively weak and hesitant. This is shown primarily in the fact that industrial production has had difficulty rising back to the highest levels it had attained on the eve of the recession (see Table 23).

Table 23

Industrial Production at the End of 1976 Compared to Before the Recession
(100 = 1970)

Country	Maximum before recession	4th quarter 1976
United States	September 1973: 123	November: 123
Japan	March 1974: 139	October: 130
West Germany	November 1975: 125	November: 117
Britain	November 1973: 117	October: 109
France	November 1973: 136	October: 130
Italy	October 1973: 136	November: 130

Source: OECD.

Even more important, however, the recovery has been too limited to reabsorb unemployment. For the international bourgeoisie, the 'historic function' of the 1974–75 recession was precisely to put an end to 'full employment' as the 'priority objective of economic, monetary, and social policy'[4] and to reintroduce permanent and massive unemployment to weigh on the 'labour market'. From this standpoint, the 1976 Nobel

[4] That this was a matter of ideological mystification in any event is proven by the fact that genuine full employment has practically never been achieved under the capitalist system, except in time of war. What is usually called 'full employment' is an unemployment rate less than 2%, 3%, or 4% of the work force or active population, depending on the country.

Prize for Economics awarded to Milton Friedman was the symbol of the 'anti-Keynesian counter-revolution' that has occurred in bourgeois economic ideology. This 'counter-revolution' reflects a shift in the socio-economic priorities of the capitalist class both materially and in terms of class struggle.

Indeed, the official spokesman of the international bourgeoisie, as well as bourgeois representatives of academic science, are not mincing words in this regard. Professor Karl Brunner, a leading Swiss monetarist now living in the United States, has asserted: 'If we want to eliminate inflation there will be a price to pay, and that price is unemployment. Unemployment is therefore the social cost of putting an end to inflation. And don't come and tell me there's another way out, because it's not true.' One of the world's leading monetarists, the recently deceased Professor Harry G. Johnson, expressed himself no less coarsely: 'The answer [to inflation] depends . . . in the long run . . . on the will of society to turn away from the Welfare State.'[5]

A bit more coyly, but hardly less clearly, the authors of the forty-seventh annual report of the Bank for International Settlements affirmed: 'This report is rather in sympathy with the current of thought which maintains that the acceleration of inflation during the sixties and the beginning of the seventies resulted in large part from the asserted desire of authorities to maintain full employment, while the potential effects of the tightening of job markets and the shortage of capacities on price stability were neglected.'[6]

Finally, Claassen and Salin, expressing themselves even more prudently in highly politicized France, write: 'The struggle against inflation requires a restrictive monetary policy such that monetary growth becomes that much closer to the predicted rate of real GNP growth the more rapidly a return to stability is desired. The risk of this policy is obviously the aggravation of unemployment.'[7]

[5] *Tendances/Trends*, 8 September 1976; *The Banker*, August 1975.
[6] *47e Rapport Annuel de la Banque des Reglements Internationaux*, p. 51.
[7] op. cit., p. 86.

There could be no better confirmation of the analysis Marx presented in *Capital* more than a century ago: in the long run, capitalism cannot survive without an industrial reserve army, in other words, without unemployment. All the right-thinking Social Democrats and other reformists who claimed that the 'mixed economy' under which we are said to be living was no longer a capitalist economy have once again been rebuked for their trouble.

The 1974–75 recession left a 'residue' of structural unemployment which the OECD evaluated at 15.5 million for all the imperialist countries at the end of 1976. At the end of 1977 the same organization estimated that unemployment in the member countries (all the imperialist countries) had risen to 16.3 million. It predicted a new increase for 1978, the number of officially unemployed workers approaching 17 million. Table 24 indicates the breakdown by country.

Table 24

Evolution of Unemployment During the Recovery
(number of unemployed in thousands)

Country	September 1976	December 1977
United States	7,400	6,337
Britain	1,319	1,428
Italy	1,145	1,558
Japan	1,130	1,140
West Germany	890	1,027
France	841	1,027
Spain	750	1,000
Canada	775	912
Benelux	444	555
Australia	350	400

Sources: Government statistics, except for Spain, for which I have used the estimates of economic reviews.

Now, at the worst point of the recession there were 17 million unemployed. In other words, unemployment has been practically unaffected by a recovery that has nonetheless increased industrial production by an average of 10% compared with the worst point of the recession. Such is the eloquent balance-sheet of the period 1973–78 as far as employment is concerned.

The decline in employment of youth, women, and immigrant workers, i.e. the most vulnerable and economically weakest sectors of the proletariat, has been especially dramatic. 18% of youth in the United States who had completed their studies were jobless as of July 1976. For blacks between the ages of 16 and 19 the unemployment rate was 34.1%. At the beginning of 1977 more than half the 7 million officially registered unemployed workers in the United States were less than 24 years old. The evolution of unemployment of youth as a percentage of total unemployment in the Common Market countries was as shown in Table 25.

Table 25

Number of Unemployed Youth as % of Total Unemployed

	Belgium	France	West Germany	Italy	Britain
1967	16.3	19.4	12.2	22.8	25.9
1970	11.9	23.1	18.7	26.5	27.3
1972	17.2	25.0	19.8	27.3	31.7
1975	31.5	37.4	28.6	34.1	41.9
1976	33.3	37.7	24.8[a]	—	43.9
1977[c]	43.5	46.0	26.6[b]	39.0	45.5

[a] September 1976
[b] May 1977
[c] September 1977

Source: EEC statistics.

For the EEC as a Whole

	as % of total unemployed	in absolute figures
1969–73 (average)	26.5	561,000
1974	30.7	824,000
1975	35.3	1,512,000
1976	37.0	1,778,000
1977	37.4	1,996,000

Source: Eurostat.

In France 54.5% of unemployed workers as of September 1977 were women. The unemployment rate among women in West Germany was 5.9% at the end of 1976, as against 3.4% for men. The gap was even greater in the Ruhr: 6.6% to 3.4%. In Belgium the rate was 12.5% for women and 6.7% for men as of 1976.

The rate of unemployment of immigrant workers in West Germany in September 1975 was 7.3%, as against 4.3% for all wage earners. If the rate has declined since then, it is because some 550,000 of these workers – 20% of the total – had been sent back to their countries of origin by the end of 1976.[8]

3. A Hesitant and Inflationary Recovery

Once the causes for the turn in the cycle are examined, it becomes evident that the recession was halted and the upturn initiated by enormous budget deficits in 1975–76. This means that in the course of 1975 and 1976 there was a reversal in the tendency of private debt to grow more rapidly than public debt, which is normal during a phase of relative stagnation of business and greater abundance of money-capital in the hands of big capital. Because of the conjunction of the rise in the rate of profit, the greater liquidity of trusts, and the very slow upturn of their investments, recourse to bank loans declined, while the public debt was soaring.[9]

At first sight it may seem paradoxical to speak of an inflationary recovery when everyone has been emphasizing the slowdown in the rate of price increases. This slowdown was real in 1976 and 1977 if the rate of inflation in those years is compared with the rate of 1973 and 1974. But it is no longer real if the 1976–77 inflation rate is compared with the average annual rates of the sixties. Such a comparison clearly shows that the inflation rate remains generally higher than that which prevailed in all the imperialist countries after the end of the

[8] Winfried Wolf, op. cit., pp. 125–26.

[9] There are, however, exceptions. In Belgium bank credit to the private sector rose from 300 thousand million francs at the beginning of 1972 to 782 thousand million francs at the end of 1976. It increased faster than credit to the public sector, which rose from 235 thousand million francs to 447 thousand million francs during the same period.

Second World War. Indeed, the cost of living and prices of consumer goods continued to rise, even in the midst of the recession – despite a sharp decline in the price scales of nearly all raw materials, a collapse in the prices of some manufactured products, the re-emergence of fierce price competition in some sectors (such as textiles and electrical appliances), and a generalized over-production of nearly all finished products (see Table 26).

Table 26

Average Annual Increase in Cost of Living (in %)

Country	Average, 1959–60/ 1972–73	1974	1975	1976	1977
United States	2.6	11.4	8.0	5.8	6.5
West Germany	3.3	7.0	5.8	4.5	3.9
Japan	6.0	4.4	11.8	10.4	8.0
France	4.5	13.7	11.8	9.7	9.5
Britain	4.1	15.1	21.5	15.8	15.9
Italy	4.6	19.1	16.8	16.6	18.2^a
Canada	2.6	10.5	11.0	7.5	8.0
Netherlands	5.0	10.0	10.5	9.0	6.7
Sweden	4.6	9.9	9.5	9.5	11.4

^{a} From October 1976 to October 1977.

Sources: *Economic Outlook*, OECD, November 1975; *Perspectives économiques de l'OCDE*, December 1977; OECD press statement, 9 February 1978.

It is true that there was a pronounced slowdown in inflation in Britain and Italy during the third quarter of 1977. In Japan there was even a 3.5% decline in the cost of living during the fourth quarter as a result of the decline in the cost of imports consequent upon the constant revaluation of the yen. But the general trend is no less clear.

The inflationary character of the recovery confronts international capitalism, and particularly the bourgeois governments, be they right or left, with a dilemma which is especially painful in those countries with higher than average inflation rates. The governments of these countries can either continue to give priority to the 'struggle against inflation' or they can abstain from any deflationary measures and continue the 1975–76 pattern of stimulating the recovery through significant budget deficits, cheap credit, and an increase in the money supply in general. If they opt for the former policy, then any 'excessive' inflation rate (meaning one higher than the international average of imperialist countries) must be answered with severe deflationary measures that would interrupt the recovery and plunge the economy back into the recession from which it has barely emerged. This is what occurred in Britain, where companies have had to pay up to 20% interest for short-term loans, and in Italy and France (after the initiation of the 'Barre plan'). In all three of these countries, industrial production declined in absolute terms after the deflationary measures were taken.

If the bourgeois governments opt for the second policy, i.e. abstention from deflationary measures, then inflation must inevitably intensify. This has occurred in the United States and Sweden. West Germany and Japan have escaped this development so far only because of the moderation of the stimulatory measures and because of the initial incidence of the rise in the exchange rates of their currencies.[10] But the only result is a much slower recovery than anticipated, one that threatens to halt at a certain threshold. Going further would require more energetic 'pump priming', which is what was done in the United States, and the price for that would be a new acceleration of inflation.

The 'fiscal crisis of the state' also sets objective limits on the increase in budget deficits and the recovery measures, if a plunge into galloping inflation is to be averted. As we have already stressed, in most countries the recovery measures of 1975 and 1976 were accompanied by an enormous increase in the public debt. This was the price paid for averting a catastrophic

[10] In the longer run these modifications in exchange rates threaten to have contrary effects, particularly if the central banks of these countries, in their efforts to defend the competitive position of their exports, begin buying dollars massively, which entails a swelling of the money supply. The money supply already rose more strongly in 1977 in West Germany and Japan (10%) than in the United States (7.5%).

crisis of the scope of the 1929–32 depression and for the effort to transform it into a recession more limited in depth and breadth, albeit the most serious since the Second World War. Everywhere important sectors of the bourgeoisie are exerting constant pressure for a slowdown in the rate of increase of public spending and budget deficits.[11]

The scope of the budget deficits, and of the resulting increase in the public debt, may be measured by the fact that as of 1975 they amounted to 5% of GNP in the United States, 7% in West Germany, and 9% in Britain. The same remark applies even more strongly to the smaller imperialist countries, such as Norway, Sweden, and Austria, where Social Democratic governments had succeeded in strictly limiting the extent of the 1974–75 recession.[12]

The 'socio-economic performance' of these governments was certainly better than average, both as concerns defence of employment and as concerns maintenance of the real income of the workers. This may be explained essentially by the special manner in which these countries are integrated into the world market.[13] In the case of Austria there is an additional, subsidiary factor: the scope of the nationalized sector of the economy, the highest of any imperialist country; and Norway was temporarily aided by its large oil resources. The accumulation of significant reserves also permitted a more audacious anti-cyclical policy without provoking double-digit inflation. The growth of the public debt was nevertheless striking in these countries (Table 27). It is thus unlikely that they will be able to repeat this performance during the next recession.

---

[11] This campaign includes a good dose of demagogy. It is precisely during periods of crisis that the employers more than ever address themselves to the public authorities for aid in reflating. What the capitalists demand is not so much a reduction as a restructuring of public spending: less social spending, more subsidies to the private sector, and more military spending (and therefore more state orders).

[12] The Norwegian government had to shift to a deflationary policy at the end of 1977, despite the fact that industrial production proper had already dropped 1% in 1977. It will probably continue to decline in 1978.

[13] In the case of Sweden, one must remember that the industrial cycle in this country is still somewhat out of phase with the international cycle. See Benny Asman in *Inprecor*, no. 48–49, 24 December 1975.

Table 27

Evolution of the Public Debt in Austria
(in thousands of millions of current schillings)

Year	Debt	As % of GNP
1972	49.8	10.62
1973	56.2	10.55
1974	61.3	10.00
1975	100.3	15.34
1976	134.2	18.52
1977 (forecast)	165.6	20.5

Source: *Die Presse*, 22 October 1976.

The major characteristic of the recovery, however, was its *unevenness by country and sector, and hence its non-cumulative and hesitant character.* It is important to analyse the causes of this phenomenon, and to emphasize the major features of this jerky recovery, which was unable really to take off.

(1) *The upturn of productive investment was much slower than expected* and did not succeed in stimulating household consumption sufficiently to provide a foundation for the recovery (Table 28). This was not a result of insufficient profits, as we have already demonstrated. It was due essentially to the *pressure of unused productive capacities,* which at the end of 1977, in the midst of the recovery, continued to fluctuate around 20% for the imperialist countries as a whole, even in the United States, where the recovery was strongest. Significant in this regard is the commentary in *Business Week,* eloquently entitled 'Where is the capital spending boom?': 'In the US capital spending is still running some 9% below the peak reached more than two and a half years ago, in the second half of 1973. In Japan capital spending is some 24% below the rate of the late 1973 period. In the four major countries of Western Europe – Germany, Britain, France, and Italy – the shortfall is some 11%. And if the US seems to be mounting the most successful capital spending recovery of any of the advanced countries, growth in it is still slower this year than in any of

the five earlier postwar recoveries.'[14]

Table 28

Comparison, by Cycle, of the Evolution of Non-residential Investments
(as % of preceding peak)

(The Roman numerals indicate the four quarters of each year.)

West Germany	II/1966–I/1969	+ 11.8
	III/1971–II/1974	− 6.5
	I/1974–IV/1976	+ 7.4
Canada	I/1960–IV/1962	+ 5.1
	I/1969–IV/1971	+ 14.9
	I/1974–IV/1976	+ 0.5
United States	I/1960–II/1963	+ 9.0
	IV/1969–I/1973	+ 12.5
	IV/1973–I/1977	− 7.9
France	I/1964–I/1966	+ 15.8
	II/1966–II/1968	+ 12.2
	III/1974–III/1976	+ 4.1
Japan	I/1962–I/1965	+ 31.7
	IV/1964–IV/1967	+ 40.4
	IV/1973–IV/1976	− 12.9
Britain	IV/1964–I/1968	+ 17.0
	II/1969–III/1972	+ 8.8
	III/1973–IV/1976	− 13.9

Source: Bank for International Settlements, *47e Rapport Annuel.*

It is not surprising that under these conditions there was an abundance of money-capital, and companies resorted to bank credit only very moderately. Indeed, on the week ending 29 September 1976 bank credit to American companies totalled $116.6 thousand million, as against $123.5 thousand million at the end of September 1975. In other words, there was a 5.5% *decline*, which is equivalent to a 10% decline if inflation is taken into account. One year later, on 28 September 1977, the volume of these loans stood at $125 thousand million, scarcely exceeding the 1975 total. Once again, taking account of inflation, this represents about a 12% decline in the volume of credit in real terms.

[14] 1 November 1975.

The same phenomenon has been noted in Britain: 'Caution is leading to an important reduction in recourse to bank loans. According to a statement by Anthony Rudge, president of the local board of Barclays Bank in Birmingham, firms in the metal industry are taking only some 38% of the volume of advances in current accounts that are offered them.'[15]

(2) *Demand for consumer goods on the domestic market was no longer rising* after it acted to 'detonate' the recovery (Table 29). The cumulative movement was interrupted as a result of persistent unemployment and inflation, the lack of an investment boom, and in some countries the deflationary measures that rapidly followed the recovery measures.

Table 29

Purchasing Power of the Masses in the Major Imperialist Countries in 1975

Country	Rise in real net income (in %)	Rise in savings rate (%)	Rise in volume of consumption
United States	1.4	0.7	0.7
West Germany	4.4	2.3	2.1
Japan	2.9	−1.1	4.0
France	3.0	1.1	1.9
Britain	0.2	0.6	−0.4
Canada	2.3	0.4	1.9
Italy	0.9	3.4	−2.5

Source: OECD, *Economic Outlook*, no. 18, December 1975, p. 24.

As may be seen, the volume of domestic consumption increased only in the most moderate proportions (except in Japan), and this despite the massive budget deficits. As a whole, the volume of retail sales (at fixed prices) in the United States increased only 3% between September 1975 and September 1976, and less than 3% between September 1976 and September 1977, despite the fact that the volume of employment rose 5% during these two years and the disposable income in real terms rose 10%. The stagnation in the volume of domestic consumption was even more pronounced in Britain, where, calculating

[15] *The Observer*, 10 October 1976.

on the basis of 1970 fixed prices, it stood during the second quarter of 1976 at a level slightly lower than that of the annual average of 1973.

(3) *The recovery was uneven internationally.* Although the imperialist countries plunged into recession simultaneously in 1974 and 1975, the recovery was not simultaneous, nor of equal scope everywhere. On the whole the international mechanism of recovery functioned as follows:

(a) Upturn of production in the United States as of the second quarter of 1975, stimulated in particular by a strong recovery of the automobile industry (the construction industry, second major detonator of the crisis, took a long time recovering, remaining in a slump throughout 1975 and 1976).[16]

(b) Recovery in Japan and West Germany, in some EEC countries and in countries like Austria and Switzerland that are closely dependent on the EEC. But while the German and Japanese recoveries continued to be fuelled by exports throughout 1976 and the beginning of 1977, there was a sudden interruption of the recovery in France and the Benelux countries during the second half of 1976, caused by the weaker competitive position of their exported products, a rise in the prices of their exports greater than that of West German exports and government deflationary measures to combat the acceleration of inflation. (In Belgium and Luxembourg the effects of the serious crisis of the steel industry also played a role.)

(d) In Britain the recovery was slower from the outset, and in Italy it was of shorter duration. In both cases it was completely strangled by the severe deflationary measures taken by the governments.

(e) A very important fact: the American expansion of 1976 and the beginning of 1977 was not accompanied by a proportional upturn in imports, either from the imperialist countries

---

[16] The continued stagnation of construction in the United States at the beginning of the recovery was due to the dizzying increase in prices. The price of a new, single-family house hit $43,600 in autumn 1976, *twice the average 1970 price*. Likewise, the price of a new apartment in Paris rose 48% between 1974 and the middle of 1976 (*Le Monde*, 28 September 1976). It is therefore not surprising that the rate of construction in France in 1977 remained 15% lower than during the second half of 1974.

(with the exception of Japan) or from the semi-colonial and dependent countries. Indeed, during the nine months from the end of the third quarter of 1975 to the end of the first half of 1976, the total exports of the EEC countries rose 16.4%, but their exports to the United States *diminished* 5.5%. During the same period, Japanese exports to the United States increased by 40%.

Experts on this matter believed that growth within the three most powerful imperialist economies – the United States, West Germany, and Japan – would have the effect of stimulating growth in the other imperialist countries. But the performance of each of these countries has been different (Table 30), as has the performance of each sector of the international imperialist economy.

Table 30

1% increase in aggregate demand in:	*Provokes a GNP growth in:*			*Leading to growth in other European countries of:*
	United States	*Japan*	*West Germany*	
United States	2.0%	0.35%	0.50%	0.35%
Japan	0.1%	00%	00%	0.15%
West Germany	0.05%	0.10%	1.60%	0.30%

Source: OECD, *Economic Outlook*, no. 18, December 1975, p. 34.

Competition and mutual dependence – these are the factors that govern relations among the imperialist powers. But since the law of uneven development continues to operate and since the relationship of forces shifts constantly, the *precise* repercussions of varying growth rates and varying economic policies in each imperialist power on its competitors/partners and on the international economic situation as a whole are incalculable and unpredictable.

(4) *The recovery was uneven by sector.* This was a result of the combined influence of the varying rates of excess capacity in the different sectors and the increasingly diverse medium- and long-term evolution of demand in each sector.

For instance, the automobile industry, along with the machine construction industry, had been the major 'detonator' of the recovery. Its growth rate, however, did not match the record figures of the fifties and sixties. This industry was therefore unable to 'carry' the recovery into a rapid and lasting expansion. Automobile sales in the United States are expected to level off, or even decline, as of 1978.

The boom in the steel industry had terminated at the end of 1974. There was a recovery at the beginning of 1976, but another recession broke out in autumn 1976. This recession worsened throughout 1977. The persistence of this crisis was determined by the decline in traditional outlets for this industry in countries which are now beginning to satisfy their own demands, as well as by the slump in construction and ship-building, two big customers of the steel industry. The former phenomenon is indicated in Table 31.

The textile industry was also experiencing a slump of greater duration. The chemical industry has performed in a more differentiated manner during the recovery, the petrochemicals sector (especially synthetic fibres) suffering acute excess capacity on a world scale, the other sectors of this branch participating more vigorously in the rise of industrial production. The machine construction industry (especially the 'ready-made factories' sector), the electrical construction industry, electronics, and the energy sector (including energy equipment) were all fully participating in the recovery.

Graph 3, taken from *The Oriental Economist*, strikingly reflects the varied intensity of the recovery in the different branches of industry. The magazine made this comment: 'Such a wide gap in the pace of recovery by different industries, which was not witnessed in the past periods of business recovery, is attributable to the unique pattern of the latest rally. The brisk increase of export trade has taken the leadership of the latest business recovery, as under similar circumstances in the past. However, inventory and plant-equipment investments, which followed suit in previous periods, have not made a tangible rally after domestic business hit bottom about one year before.'

The conclusion that must be drawn from these four factors is

Table 31

Evolution of International Steel Production (in millions of tonnes)

	1974	*1975*	*1976*	*1977*(§)
Group A				
USSR	136.2	141.3	144.8	147.0
China	25.0	26.5	21.0	23.4
Poland	14.6	15.0	15.3	18.0
Czechoslovakia	13.6	14.3	14.7	15.0
Group B				
United States	132.0	106.0	116.3	113.1
Japan	117.1	102.3	107.4	102.4
West Germany	53.2	40.4	42.4	39.0
Italy	23.8	21.9	23.5	23.3
France	27.0	21.5	23.2	22.1
Britain	22.4	19.8	22.5	20.4
Canada	13.6	13.0	13.2	13.7
Belgium	16.2	11.6	12.1	—
Spain	11.5	11.1	11.0	—
Sweden	6.0	5.6	5.1	—
Australia	7.8	7.9	7.8	—
Group C				
India	7.1	8.0	9.4	—
Brazil	7.5	8.4	9.2	—
Mexico	5.1	5.3	5.3	—
South Korea	1.9	2.0	3.5	—
Taiwan	0.9	1.0	1.6	—
Rumania	8.8	9.5	10.5	—

§ Provisional figures.

Source: *Neue Zürcher Zeitung*, 18 January 1977; *Financial Times*, 25 January 1978.

clear: there could not be a rapid and cumulative recovery leading to a new boom. The fragmented, hesitant, and uneven recovery constantly borders on a plunge into a new recession. Compared with the long wave of expansion of the fifties and sixties, today's recessions and recoveries remain dominated by a *general depression of growth factors*.[17]

[17] This is not *post facto* sagacity: 'One of the major features of the present economic upturn is its hesitant and non-cumulative character. . . . The upturn is uneven internationally and by sector' (*Inprecor*, no. 60–62, 11 November

Graph 3
Business Recovery and Production Activity

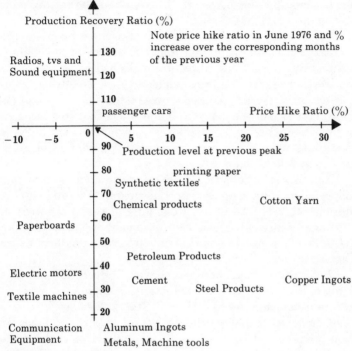

Production Recovery Ratio (%)

Note price hike ratio in June 1976 and % increase over the corresponding months of the previous year

Radios, tvs and Sound equipment

130
120
110

passenger cars

Price Hike Ratio (%)

-10   -5   0   5   10   15   20   25   30

90   Production level at previous peak

80   printing paper
     Synthetic textiles
70
     Chemical products   Cotton Yarn
60
Paperboards
50
     Petroleum Products
40
Electric motors
     Cement   Copper Ingots
30   Steel Products
Textile machines
20
Communication   Aluminum Ingots
Equipment   Metals, Machine tools

Production recovery Ration
Production Level at previous peak
Price Hike Ratio

Source: *The Oriental Economists*, September 1976.

4. The New Protectionism

The uneven character of the recovery in the various imperialist countries inevitably intensified the inter-imperialist com-

---

1976). And in no. 40–41 of the same magazine (18 December 1975) I had written: 'The conclusion is clear: the recession will not lead to a powerful boom, but to a limited upturn leading rather rapidly to a new recession.' The opposing forecasts of the OECD experts, who in December 1975 were still predicting an average annual growth rate of 6% through the end of the seventies, not to mention those of *The Economist*, which spoke of a 'new boom' (issue of 12 April 1975), proved to be rather fanciful.

petitive struggle, even though this unevenness itself resulted in part from the preceding aggravation of competition, which led to a modification of the relative weight of the various powers in the international capitalist market.

The most pronounced feature of this new phase of inter-imperialist competition has been the growing recourse to protectionist practices. These practices had never disappeared entirely, of course, but they had clearly waned during the long period of post-war economic expansion. It is a notorious characteristic of the history of capitalism that free trade rises primarily during euphoric phases of expansion, while the pro-tectionist temptation surfaces primarily under conditions of protracted depression.

Examples of protectionist measures taken by the major imperialist countries during the years 1976 and 1977 are innumerable. No less than 800 complaints were presented to the 1977 conference of the General Agreement on Tariffs and Trade (GATT). Here we will mention only a few particularly flagrant instances:

– Under the guise of an agreement on 'orderly marketing' the United States imposed a reduction in Japanese exports of colour televisions to the United States. Similar agreements were imposed to reduce the growth of imports of shoes from South Korea and Taiwan. An initial application of the 'orderly marketing arrangement' struck imports of special steel products to the United States in 1976.

– At the end of 1977 the EEC imposed restrictive quotas on the import of textile products from Hong Kong, South Korea, and other Asian countries in the context of the renewal of the so-called multifibre agreement.[18]

– Under the cover of the struggle against dumping, the United States sought to impose limits on the import of steel products from both Japan and Europe. (The so-called Solomon

---

[18] The multifibre agreement called for a 6% yearly increase in the import of textile products into the EEC countries during 1974–77. During the difficult negotiations aimed at extending this agreement for another four years, the EEC actually reduced import quotas 9% for Hong Kong and 7% for South Korea.

Project, moreover, would affect European products more strongly than Japanese.)

– Italy ordered provisional taxes on imports (including imports from EEC members) so as to eliminate the balance of payments deficit.

– France reduced imports of Italian shoes.

– Italy resorted to massive import restrictions on textile products, not only those coming from the countries of the East and the 'third world' but also those from European countries that are not members of the EEC (Switzerland, Portugal, and Turkey were special targets).

– The EEC imposed exorbitant customs charges on the import of metallic screws and motor-cycle chains from Taiwan and on the import of ball-bearings from Japan.

– Ceding to the 'sugar lobby', the United States imposed an entry fee on foreign sugar amounting to 60% of the current price of sugar on the world market (it should be noted that the price of sugar collapsed from 30 cents a pound in 1975 to less than 10 cents a pound in November 1977 and that the present production costs of sugar in the United States are reported to be about 13–14 cents a pound).

– The EEC took severe measures to limit import of steel products at the end of 1977, decreeing minimum prices for imported goods.

– Japan limited the import of some rare European articles that had effectively conquered the Japanese market, such as Italian and French ski boots.

– Canada reduced 1978 import allowances for textile products from the 'third world' to their 1975 levels.

– Australia multiplied its protectionist practices.

– Sweden radically reduced its imports of Italian shoes, which led to the retaliatory measure of EEC limits on the import of Swedish paper.[19]

Even though the overall scope of all these protectionist measures remains modest for the moment, the general trend is

---

[19] The 21 January 1978 *Frankfurter Rundschau* published a table of the protectionist offensive that has been under way since 1974–75.

disquieting to the international bourgeoisie. The bourgeoisie fears, and correctly so, that a broader and broader return to protectionism would entail a lasting contraction of the volume of world trade similar to that of the thirties, with disastrous effects on the economic cycle as a whole.

'There is a strong whiff of protectionism in the air,' wrote *The Economist* in April 1977. In the view of *Business Week*, the Carter administration's pressure in favour of 'orderly marketing' amounted in reality to the formation of cartels and to indirect protectionism. In *Le Monde* Pierre Drouin emphasized that the 'industrial nations' were falling victim to 'the protectionist temptation'. Italian Minister of Foreign Trade Ossola openly called for more long-term protectionism for his country in order to reduce imports on a lasting basis.[20].

The results of all this were not long in coming. During the third quarter of 1977, for the first time since the end of the recession, the volume of world trade (or at least of international capitalist trade, excluding exchanges among non-capitalist countries) *began to contract again*. The figures are indicated in Table 32.

Table 32

Contraction of World Trade Between the Second and Third Quarters of 1977 (in thousands of millions of dollars)

All capitalist countries	*Imports*	*Exports*
3rd quarter 1976	155.7	144.7
2nd quarter 1977	182.8	170.7
3rd quarter 1977	166.3	155.3
	2nd quarter 1977	*3rd quarter 1977*
United States	31.6	28.7
West Germany	28.8	28.3
Japan	19.7	20.6
France	16.7	14.6
Britain	14.2	14.6

Source: International Monetary Fund.

[20] *The Economist*, 23 April 1977; *Business Week*, 9 May 1977; *Le Monde*, 8 January 1977; *Neue Zürcher Zeitung*, 11 May 1977.

These figures underscore and extend the trends we noted in section 9. These may be seen even more clearly if the evolution of manufactured goods from 1975 to 1977 is examined (Table 33).

Table 33

Share of the Major Imperialist Powers in World Exports of Manufactured Products (in % of total)

	United States	West Germany	Japan	France	Italy	Britain
1964	21.5	19.3	8.1	8.7	6.3	14.4
1970	18.5	19.8	11.7	8.7	7.2	10.8
1974	17.2	21.7	14.5	9.3	6.7	8.8
1975	17.7	20.3	13.6	10.2	7.5	9.3
1976	17.4	20.7	14.6	9.6	7.0	8.8
1977 (3rd quarter)	16.5	20.5	15.4	9.1	6.9	9.8

Source: *National Institute Economic Review*, November 1976. We have calculated the percentages for the third quarter of 1977 on the basis of OECD statistics.

This table clearly shows that the U.S. share of the world market in the products of manufacturing industry is being increasingly whittled down by West Germany and Japan, while Britain is making a relative comeback at the expense of France and the minor imperialist countries.

The regression of the United States is not primarily a result of its greater than expected dependence on oil imports (which is the usual explanation for the mounting U.S. balance of payments deficit). Rather, it results from the much slower rise in the productivity of industrial labour in the United States and from the lower rate of investment, i.e. the obsolescence of the American apparatus of production compared with that of the major U.S. competitors (Tables 34 and 35). West Germany and France have even managed to penetrate a sector of the world market that had been considered an exclusive American preserve not long ago: the export of electro-nuclear materials. Much of the 'humanitarian' noise Jimmy Carter has made about the dangers of the proliferation of nuclear weapons can be explained more prosaically by his desire to reduce the

Table 34

Average Annual Rate of Growth of Productivity of Labour (Output per Hour)
in Manufactures

	United States	Japan	West Germany	France	Italy	Britain
1960–1975	2.7%	9.7%	5.7%	5.6%	6.2%	3.8%
1970–1975	1.8%	5.4%	5.4%	3.4%	6.0%	3.1%

Source: US Department of Labour, Bureau of Labour Statistics, Bulletin No. 1958, Washington DC, 1977.

Table 35

Rates of Investment (as % of GNP)

	Annual average 1970–74	1975	1976	1977 (est.)
United States	18.8	15.6	17.1	18.4
West Germany	24.9	20.8	20.8	21.1
Japan	34.9	30.8	29.9	32.3
France	23.8	23.3	23.1	22.7
Italy	20.9	20.8	20.3	20.2
Britain	19.1	19.9	19.0	17.9
Belgium	21.8	20.7	21.4	20.9
Netherlands	24.0	21.3	19.8	20.6
Sweden	22.0	20.9	20.5	19.9
Austria	28.1	26.7	26.0	26.5

Source: *Notices Economiques* of the Union de Banques Suisses, November 1977.

preponderant position such exports are beginning to acquire in the domain of energy, with the huge orders the West German and French nuclear industries have won on the Brazilian, Iranian, and South African markets (and perhaps on the Chinese market in the future).[21]

[21] After the visit of U.S. Secretary of State Cyrus Vance to Brasilia in November 1977, the Carter administration withdrew its opposition to the operation of Brazilian nuclear power plants. A veritable sharing out of the 'Brazilian nuclear market' between American and European trusts laid the basis for this compromise (see especially *Le Monde*, 23 November 1977).

There have been other sensational 'breakthroughs' by competitors of U.S. imperialism as well: the most technologically advanced aeronautic prototypes (Concorde, as well as the French helicopter Astar, which is extensively penetrating the U.S. market); tyre technology (Michelin); electrical appliances. Moreover, it appears that an international cartel – essentially Anglo-French, dominated by Rio Tinto Zinc – has managed to raise the world market price of uranium from $6 in 1973 to $30–40 during the third quarter of 1976, a higher increase than that for oil. We have already mentioned the sensational breakthroughs of the 'big three' Japanese exports on North American and West European markets (colour televisions, automobiles, and air conditioning apparatuses).

The great multinational corporations, apparently caught in the vice of the aggravation of international competition on the one hand and the rise of protectionism on the other hand, have reacted to the recession and the hesitant recovery in two different ways:

(1) *They have further shifted their production centres to countries in which they enjoy low wages.* In this regard one must note not only the mounting capital exports of Japan to East and Southeast Asia and of the United States to Mexico and the Far East, but also the sharp rise in the establishment of new companies or the absorption of existing ones in the United States by the great European multinationals. The most spectacular initiatives in this regard have been taken by British Petroleum, Volkswagen, Michelin, Saint Gobin, Fiat, Siemens, Unilever, Philips, Air Liquide, and British Oxygen, all of which have either bought or constructed large enterprises in the United States. One American multinational, Allis-Chambers, has been literally 'dismembered' by the European multinationals, Fiat taking over the road-construction machinery department of this trust, Siemens the heavy electrical and regulatory equip-

According to *Business Week* (26 December 1977), the Hague factory in France will be the sole commercially viable reprocessing installation during the coming decade. Some European consortiums are well-placed for the production of fast breeder reactors and rapid sodium reactors.

ment department.[22]

It is true that the entire process of expansion by the multi-nationals into dependent countries cannot be reduced to their search for lower wage costs. It also corresponds in part – especially in Latin America and partially in South Korea – to the re-employment of equipment and/or technology already obsolete in the countries in which large-scale, assembly-line production holds sway. This equipment and technology can be used longer at a profit where the markets are narrower.[23]

As we have long stressed, the constant devaluation of the dollar relative to the yen, the deutschmark, and the Swiss franc is a two-edged sword. While it undoubtedly favours exports of American *commodities* (although with mediocre results, as we have seen), it simultaneously facilitates the export of European (especially West German) and Japanese capital to the United States. In practice, a West German or Swiss investor today has to lay out 40% fewer deutschmarks or Swiss francs, a Japanese trust 30% fewer yen, to buy a firm in the United States priced in American dollars.

The direct foreign investments of West Germany and Japan have consequently *increased sevenfold* since 1967. In that year they amounted to only 7% of total American direct foreign investment; the figure had risen to 20% by 1975 and 35% by 1977. If to this is added the foreign investments of Britain, France, and the Netherlands, European and Japanese foreign investment attains some 70% of total American foreign investment. *North American imperialism is thus beginning to lose its*

[22] Siemens also absorbed Advanced Micro Devices and, together with Corning Glass Works, established Siecor Optical Cables Inc. The German Thyssen trust absorbed the Budd Company, one of the major American firms supplying parts for the automobile industry. In 1977 the total value of the major American companies absorbed by British trusts was more than $900 million. The most spectacular cases were the absorption of National Starch and Chemical by Unilever, of the Calgon division of Merck by the Beecham group, of Airco by EOC, and of Milgon Electronics by Racal Electronics.

[23] I had already indicated this phenomenon in *Late Capitalism*. Our friend Pierre Salama develops it in great detail and in a highly subtle analysis, in an article entitled 'Spécificités de l'Internationalisation du Capital en Amérique latine', to be published shortly in the review *Tiers Monde*. Salama's article is a polemic against the opposite thesis, expressed in extreme form by A. Michelet, *Le Capitalisme Mondial*, Paris, 1976.

*preponderance in the domain of capital exports, having already
lost that preponderance in the domain of the export of manufactured commodities. This is the inexorable cost of the devaluation
of the dollar.* And if this decline continues and is combined with
a persistent gap in the domain of the productivity of labour,
U.S. preponderance in the domain of finance capital, the last
remaining realm of American predominance apart from the
politico-military, will also be increasingly broken down.

The primary reason why a growing number of European
multinationals are transferring their production centres to the
United States is that wage differentials between Europe and
the United States as expressed in dollars have disappeared as a
result of modifications in exchange rates. This makes production in the United States, which reduces transport costs, more
attractive than export to the United States. The greater political
and social stability of the United States has probably also
played a role. The disappearance of wage differentials is
indicated in Table 36.

Table 36

Wage Costs per Unit Produced

	Average 1970–73	*1974*	*1975*	*1976*	*1977*
United States	5.2	11.4	7.6	5.1	6.0
West Germany	8.2	9.4	6.9	0.9	4.0
Japan	9.1	26.5	14.6	6.0	7.0
France	7.1	15.4	17.2	10.0	7.5
Britain	8.9	20.1	32.1	12.3	10.0
Italy	11.5	20.7	26.0	16.2	20.5

Source Sachverständigenrat zur Begutachtung der gesamtwirtschaftlichen
Entwicklung, *Jahresgutachten 1977–78.*

In the case of West Germany and Japan, the effects of the
revaluation of the deutschmark and the yen relative to the
dollar, of the order of 60% and 30% respectively since 1970,
obviously must be added to the figures shown in the table.

(2) *They are stepping up cooperation accords, agreements, and
concentration on a European and Japanese scale.* The European

steel cartel is the most striking example, but it is not at all the only one. One can also mention the creation in mid-October 1977 of a powerful new financial group in Japan, uniting about forty industrial and commercial companies around the largest Japanese bank, Dai-Ichi Kangyo Bank. Among the participants are Ishikawa-Harima Heavy Industries, which is very powerful in shipbuilding, the Kawasaki Steel Corporation and Kawasaki Heavy Industries, Asahi Mutual Life Insurance, and the Seibu Department store. This group could become the most powerful Japanese financial group, overtaking Mitsubishi, Mitsui, Marubeni, Sanwa, Sumitomo, and the Fuji Bank. The goals of this concentration are vertical rationalization (steel, ship-building, machine construction), commercialization, and the concentration of capital necessary for undertaking large-scale projects such as the construction of nuclear power plants and the exploitation of the ocean floor. We may also mention the concentration of the Japanese synthetic fibre industry, in which only four large groups remain. In Europe the heavy electrical equipment industry has been reorganized (construction of turbines and generators), and cooperation is continuing and being consolidated in aeronautics construction, which, after the partial failure of the Concorde, has scored gains with the Airbus and is about to enter a new stage.

5. The International Monetary System and the Economic Cycle

The collapse of the Bretton Woods system, the end of the dollar's convertibility for gold, and the institutionalization of the system of 'floating exchange rates' have incontestably un-settled world trade, stimulating shifts in commercial channels. The United States, for instance, has deliberately 'played on' the fall of the dollar so as to improve the competitive position of U.S. manufactured products relative to those of West Germany and Japan. Britain did the same with the pound sterling during the sensational plunge of this currency at the beginning of 1977. Japan acted no differently in mid-1976, when massive and con-centrated raw materials purchases drove the yen's exchange rate down.

More generally, however, the system of 'floating exchange rates' imposes less 'internal discipline' and allows greater autonomy in the monetary policies of the various imperialist governments. Along with the massive emergence of petro-dollars on international monetary and financial markets, it has been *a factor maintaining and stimulating international infla-tion*, primarily (but not exclusively!) as a function of the per-sistent and growing balance of payments deficits of the United States, which year after year 'pour' thousands of millions of dollars in additional liquidity into international circuits. (The year 1975 was an exception in this, for the American balance of payments surplus had a slight deflationary effect on the international capitalist economy.)

The system of floating exchange rates strikingly expresses the contradiction between the growing internationalization of production on the one hand and the increasingly meagre and ineffective attempts by bourgeois governments to defend their freedom of action in face of this internationalization on the other hand.[24] But the negative effects are fast multiplying. During the third quarter of 1973 the central banks committed $2 thousand million in their efforts to 'control' (it would prob-ably be more accurate to say manipulate) the floating exchange rates; during the second quarter of 1977 a total of $22 thousand million was thus committed. Similarly, the differences in the inflation rates among various groups of countries have been accentuated by the float. Uncertainty about the future evolu-tion of exchange rates has also been accentuated, and this curbs investments and the expansion of exports, despite the generalization of assurances against exchange losses.[25]

It is a commonplace observation that there is a relationship

[24] 'The internationalization of capital markets, especially with the growth of Euro-currency markets and multinational corporations, has made the management of the world economy by governments and international institu-tions more and more difficult. The private sector has adjusted to this growing interdependence of the world economy; the public sector has not done so,' Robert Triffin, in *Business Week*, 3 October 1977.

[25] On the perverse effects of the system of floating exchange rates – accentua-tion of monetary instability, intensification of inflation, growing divergences of the situation in various imperialist countries, increased obstacles to the international propagation of growth – see especially: Bank for International

between the various rates of inflation in the imperialist countries and the fall in the exchange rate of their currencies compared with those of countries with the lowest inflation rates (Table 37).

Table 37

Compared Rates of Inflation and Fall of the Exchange Rate of the £ Relative to Other Imperialist Currencies, from December 1971 to July 1976, in %

Country	Rise of cost of living	Fall of £ compared to currency of country
United States	39.0	31.4
Canada	46.0	34.3
Belgium	53.3	39.3
France	54.5	35.1
West Germany	30.7	45.2
Italy	86.2	1.3
Netherlands	47.6	42.3
Sweden	47.0	36.4
Austria	65.9[a]	32.6
Spain	84.4	27.3
Norway	51.9	42.4
Denmark	55.6	39.5
Australia	42.7	46.1
Britain	89.9	—

[a] From November 1971 to May 1976.

Source: *Weekly Hansard*, No. 1049, 15–21 October 1976, p. 321.

Nevertheless, one must be careful not to establish a causal and mechanical correlation between the two sets of figures in Table 37, as neo-liberal monetarists are tempted to do. The difference between the inflation rates and the fall in the exchange rates are no more identical in the case of Britain than in the case of France, Italy, the Netherlands, and Australia.

In reality, a much more complex process is at work. First, a

Settlements, *47e Rapport Annuel*, pp. 40, 42; R. Walser in *Neue Zürcher Zeitung*, 27–28 August 1977; Professor Haberler in *Weltwirtschaftliches Archiv*, Kiel, vol. 113, 1977, no. 1; Hans Roper in *Frankfurter Allgemeine Zeitung*, 19 January 1978; and *Business Week*, 3 October 1977.

fall in the exchange rate of a national currency accentuates the inflationary trend primarily in the case of countries that are heavily dependent on imports of raw materials and foodstuffs which cannot be replaced in the short and medium term. Second, the compensatory character of the fluctuations in the dollar's exchange rate compared to that of the deutschmark or the Swiss franc remains to be demonstrated. In those cases, the differences in the inflation rates account for only a tiny fraction of the changes that have occurred in the exchange rates; it is clearly a matter of a devaluation of the dollar or a revaluation of the deutschmark and the Swiss franc, for there is no parity of purchasing power at current exchange rates.

In addition, account must be taken of the varying elasticity in demand for the goods exported by different countries, in other words, the varying composition of the export packages of the various imperialist powers. The autonomous interventions of the central banks are also a factor. The result varies considerably depending on whether they intervene massively to curb the fall in the exchange rate of the national currency (like the National Bank of Belgium, for example) or act passively (like the U.S. Federal Reserve System or the Bank of England).

Finally, it must not be forgotten that the exports of the capitalist countries are exports of *commodities* with *variable prices* sold in order to *make profits* – and this in the age of monopoly capitalism.

It is true that the world market is dominated by sharper competition than the domestic markets of the imperialist countries. But inasmuch as a number of imperialist firms have conquered oligopolist positions of power on the world market, it is possible for them to *transform fluctuations in exchange rates into widened profit margins*, at least in the short and medium term. British export prices, for instance, in no way reflect the dizzying fall of the pound's exchange rate relative to the dollar. Although a portion of this discrepancy is due to the lower productivity of British industry, another portion incontestably corresponds to this widening of profit margins (Table 38).

The emergence of petrodollars and the export offensive

Table 38

Export Prices of Products of Manufacturing Industry in Dollars (100 = 1970)

	1973	*1st quarter 1976*	*4th quarter 1976*
Britain	126.8	176.6	176
West Germany	147.0	187.0	197
Japan	141.0	167.0	182

Source: *Weekly Hansard*, no. 1049, 15–21 October 1976, p. 324. Figures for fourth quarter 1976: *National Institute Economic Review*, February 1977.

towards the countries of the 'third world' and the so-called socialist countries on the part of the imperialist countries have, moreover, been accompanied by a new *swelling of credit and international credit money*, which has been another factor in the maintenance of international inflation. We have seen that during the recession and at the beginning of the recovery the indebtedness of metropolitan capitalist firms tended to slacken on national markets, because of the upturn in the rate of profit and the rate of self-financing on the one hand and the relative stagnation of investment on the other hand.

In this context, there was a twofold, coherent reaction. On the one hand the imperialist banks sought new fields for loaning out the abundant money-capital at their disposal. On the other hand the multinationals and the trusts with heavy interests in exports sought to sell a greater share of their products in the semi-colonial and dependent countries and in the so-called socialist countries. For the capitalist system as a whole, then, the recovery has been brought about by a new inflationary expansion of credit, as was the case for the preceding boom. This time, however, the flow of credit has partially shifted from the imperialist countries to the countries mentioned above. In other words: the export-stimulated *recovery has been primarily a recovery stimulated by exported credit.*[26]

Although the Euro-dollar market has continued its brisk

[26] 'The entire *credit system*, and the over-trading, over-speculation, etc. connected with it, rests on the necessity of expanding and leaping over the barrier to circulation and the sphere of exchange. This appears more colossally,

expansion, attaining the tidy sum of $300 thousand million at the end of 1976 (about $340 thousand million at the end of 1977), the indebtedness of the semi-colonial countries to the imperialist countries has undergone an even more disquieting growth. According to *Business Week*, the sum total of these debts stood at $170 thousand million at the end of 1976, of which $70 thousand million was owed to private banks. Brazil alone owed $14 thousand million to U.S. private banks. According to *The Economist*: 'Bankers are now worried by these loans, but they kept trade flowing.' By the end of 1977 this mass of 'third world' debt to the imperialist countries had reached $250 thousand million.[27]

The mechanism that led to this debt deserves special attention. At the outset there was a relative abundance of money-capital in the hands of the big banks, particularly as a result of the influx of petrodollars and the slowdown in the expansion of credit to the great imperialist companies caused by the recession and the hesitant recovery. These banks have been progressively 'internationalized', just like the industrial multinationals. They have expanded the number of their branches abroad, where they realize a growing portion of their profits.[28]

---

classically, in the relations between peoples than in the relations between individuals. Thus e.g. the English forced to *lend* to foreign nations, in order to have them as customers. At bottom, the English capitalist exchanges doubly with *productive* English capital, (1) as himself, (2) as Yankee, etc. or in whatever other form he has placed his money' (Marx, *Grundrisse*, op. cit., p. 416).

[27] *Business Week*, 1 November 1976; *The Economist*, 4 September 1976; *Le Monde*, 'L'Année économique et sociale', 1977, p. 24.

[28] According to the report submitted to the Church commission, the share of profits of the thirteen largest U.S. banks deriving from operations abroad rose from 16.7% in 1970 to 49% in 1976. Of the six largest banks, none realized the greatest portion of its profits from foreign operations as of 1970. By 1976 five of the six realized more than 50% of their profits from such operations; among the figures were 78% for Chase Manhattan, 72% for Citicorp, and 64% for Banker's Trust New York Cor. ('International Debt, the Banks, and U.S. Foreign Policy,' a staff report prepared for the use of the Subcommittee on Foreign Economic Policy of the Committee on Foreign Relations of the U.S. Senate, U.S. Government Printing Office, Washington, 1977, p. 11. We shall refer to this subcommittee as the Church commission, after Senator Church, its chairman.) Moreover, the rate of profit for foreign operations was higher than for operations on the U.S. market. Chase Manhattan obtained 78% of its profits from foreign operations, whereas these accounted for only 48% of its holdings. Only 6% of Citicorp's holdings are in Latin America, but they provided 20% of its 1976 profits (ibid., p. 47).

They thus sought new customers, and found them in the 'third world' countries.

This increased supply of money-capital clearly corresponded to an increased demand on the part of these countries (with the exception of OPEC members), especially in view of the increase in their trade deficits as a result of the increase in oil prices and their greater need for food imports during 1973–76. It may thus be said that the credits to the semi-colonial and dependent countries are actually indirect subsidies to the great exporting trusts of the imperialist metropolises, which would have been unable to increase or even maintain the volume of their sales to these countries without this injection of additional credit.

Thus, for the most part *the private banks effected the recycling of petrodollars which international institutions and the sacrosanct 'mechanisms of the market' (i.e. the fluctuations in world trade) had been incapable of assuring by themselves.* They did so blindly, spurred on by competition, and with the exclusive aim of augmenting their own profits. The big American banks made the greatest commitments (it is reported that $75 thousand million of this 'third world' debt is owed to private banks, $50 thousand million to American banks and $25 thousand million to European and Japanese banks), but in general all the banks threw themselves heart and soul into granting loans abroad. The figure of $40 thousand million in foreign loans has been advanced for Swiss banks, an even higher figure for German ones. According to the report of the American Senate sub-committee cited above, at the end of 1976 the total foreign loans of the international private banking system (excluding inter-bank loans) stood at some $326 thousand million, of which $102 thousand million were from American banks and $202 thousand million from European, Japanese, and Canadian banks.

This expansion of private credit to the semi-colonial and dependent countries has undoubtedly facilitated some restructuring of the world market. But it has introduced a new element of instability into the system. Although the great fear in 1974 and 1975 was of a universal bank panic subsequent to the collapse of one or another major bank in the imperialist countries, in 1976 and 1977 the banking world was marked by grow-

ing fear of the possible insolvency of international debtors.[29]
One after the other, Zaire, Indonesia, Peru, and Turkey stood
on the brink of requesting a debt moratorium. (Indeed, private
banks refused to accord new credit to many countries for long
months. This was the case for Italy in 1976 and Turkey during
the second half of 1977.) This uneasiness becomes understandable if the rate of growth of the foreign debt of certain countries
is compared with their exchange reserves, and their growing
debt service charges with their normal foreign exchange
income (the sum of visible and invisible exports). The relevant
figures are in Table 39.

There is thus mounting pressure from private banks asking
that the public powers – and international public institutions –
reduce the weight of this debt and even take over some of the
'bad risks' outright. It is in this precise context that the
'Witteveen Project' must be situated, the proposal that the
International Monetary Fund establish a $10 thousand million
reserve to be placed at the disposal of the semi-colonial countries (or more exactly, of the imperialist banks which have lent
capital to the semi-colonial countries). The then president of
the U.S. Federal Reserve Board peremptorily declared that the
private banks simply could not continue to accord credit to
'third world' countries at the present rate if serious disturb-

---

[29] '. . . There was a pervasive mood of gloom and pessimism about the future
among both retail and investment bankers. Many said privately what they
would not state in public, that they had doubts about the ability of the private
financial system to sustain even the present level of international lending,
much less increase it.' (Report of the Church commission, op. cit., p. 59.) '. . . if
one country happens to suspend payment of this interest, even temporarily, or,
worse yet, if some country concludes a moratorium in good and proper form, a
whole series of banks could be affected simultaneously, which could trigger a
chain reaction. When all is said and done, it must not be forgotten that since
the growth of international bank loans has been much more rapid than the
growth of internal credit, the structure of the balances and profit and share
accounts of many banks has changed rapidly over the past several years. In
itself such a change is not necessarily dangerous, provided the organization of
the banks, especially in the domain of internal control and surveillance, were
consequently adapted. It may still be feared that the logistics will be unable to
keep up with the sudden acceleration in commercial growth at the desired rate'
(Bank for International Settlements, *47e Rapport Annuel*, op. cit., pp. 112–13).
For a more optimistic, and clearly apologetic, view, see the articles by the two
bankers in the July 1977 issue of *Foreign Affairs*.

Table 39

Evolution of Debt of 'Third World' Countries that do not Export Oil
(in thousands of millions of dollars)

	1967	1973	1974	1975	1976
Total debt	41.6	90.0	112.0	144.1	172.2
Service charges	5.8	12.9	15.8	20.8	25.6

Source: *Le Monde, L'année économique et sociale 1977*, p. 24.

Exchange Reserves as % of Imports for all Developing Countries
that do not Export Oil

1951–55	1966–70	1973	1974	1975
40.3	28.8	38.0	25.8	22.6

Source: United Nations, *Supplément à l'étude sur l'économie mondiale 1975*,
p. 284.

Debt of Some Asian Countries

	Total Debt in thousands of millions of $ (October 1976)	Debt service charges as % of currency income	
		1976	1977
Sri Lanka	0.5	22.9	—
Philippines	4.4	16.0	17
Pakistan	6.3	16.8	24
Indonesia	10.5	13.8	16.6
Thailand	1.3	14.6	—
India	10.8	13.5	—
South Korea	11.8	12.9	13.0

Source: *Far Eastern Economic Review*.

ances of the world economy were to be averted. Some mechanism for recycling petrodollars outside the private banking
system had to be found, he said.[30]

[30] *Neue Zürcher Zeitung*, 12–13 March 1977.

The case of Indonesia deserves particular attention, since this is a country which had obtained enormous additional income after 1973 because of the rise in oil prices. The Indonesian state administration is one of the most corrupt in the world. It furnishes a typical example of the process of primitive accumulation of private capital through the systematic plunder of the public revenue, the Indonesian people, and partially even foreign traders by high-ranking functionaries (mainly army officers), 'national' compradors, and foreign trusts.

The state oil company, Pertamina, under the direction of General Sutowo, threw itself into a series of branch activities that had little to do with the exploitation and sale of oil (among other things steel, chemical fertilizers, construction of hotels, operation of a private airline, etc.). The intent was to capitalize its currency surpluses. One of these subsidiary operations was the purchase, on time, of a fleet of giant oil tankers. It seems that some foreign financiers did a fairly good job on Pertamina. Tankers worth $100 million at the most at world market prices were sold to Pertamina for a grand total of $400 million. An entire army of British accountants and lawyers worked feverishly throughout 1976 to try to get to the bottom of this murky business. In the meantime, the Indonesian government halted payments to the creditors of Pertamina. In the end, the company wound up – a mere $10.5 thousand million in debt.

According to all evidence, these deals never could have been concluded without the connivance and complicity of high Indonesian functionaries and military officers. *Newsweek* published many spicy details of the degree of corruption in Indonesia. But the imperialist hypocrites overlooked one small detail: if there are corrupt politicians and officers in the semicolonial countries, they can exercise this corruption on a grand scale only because of the corrupting forces among the multinationals and the entire corrupting logic of the capitalist economy (and the money economy in general). Since the revelations of the Lockheed scandal, these corrupting practices of the imperialist multinationals should be known to everyone.[31]

---

[31] On the Pertamina affair and the general situation in Indonesia, see *News Week*, 8 November 1976, and *Far Eastern Economic Review*, 12 November 1976.

Finally, mention must be made of one additional factor of monetary disorder, the economic incidences of which are not negligible: the great *international shifts of floating capital as a result of speculation.* Here again the inherent logic of the multinational corporations, which operate simultaneously in a large number of countries with different currencies and which are therefore compelled to protect themselves against the threat of exchange losses, acts to intensify the successive monetary crises. When the multinationals anticipate a fall in the exchange rate of a given currency and therefore massively withdraw their liquid capital from the country concerned, they obviously accentuate that fall. This growing influence of the multinationals is compounded by growing social instability and fear of monetary collapse and 'social turmoil', even socialist revolution, which spur massive flights of capital. Such a flight of capital, mainly to Brazil, took place in Portugal in 1975. In 1976 it occurred in Spain, France, and Italy, to the tune of several thousand million dollars in each case. In early 1978 it recurred in Italy and France. Around the same time, the American multinationals themselves placed a growing portion of their liquid reserves in currency or deposit certificates in foreign banks.

The flight of Italian capital to Switzerland has led to the emergence of a genuine new 'industry' in Lugano: the establishment of new banks or new branches of existing banks. Generally, this is always done with the most complete discretion. But the scandal that struck the Lugano branch of the third of the 'big three' of the Swiss banking world – Crédit Suisse (Schweizerische Kreditanstalt), which is supposed to be the most conservative of the lot – threw revealing light on the interlacing of fiscal fraud, capital flight, the search for superprofits by the big bourgeoisie, and the competitive drive for lucrative investments by the big banks. What is significant here is precisely this imbrication, structurally linked to the very nature of late capitalism, and not the purely anecdotal aspect

---

A leftist point of view on the same subject is presented by Ernst Utrecht in *AMPO: Japan Asia Quarterly Review*, vol. 8, no. 3, October–December 1976.

of the Crédit Suisse scandal, or even its criminal character from the standpoint of bourgeois law itself.

Because of competition, and since the expansion of credit to 'national enterprises' had been curbed by the recession, the three biggest Swiss banks threw themselves into the London Euro-dollar market, where they rapidly outdistanced the British banks and the local branches of American banks.[32] But this expansion of their sphere of activity was accompanied by a decline in profits, which induced Crédit Suisse to seek more profitable fields of investment. The massive flight of Italian capital provided an excellent opportunity in this regard. This capital, deposited in the Lugano branch of Crédit Suisse, was used to buy into various Italian businesses. Illegal banking guarantees were often offered, despite the fact that short-term bank deposits were being used to finance long-term investments and loans. Some of the purchased businesses, however, fell on hard times as a result of the recession. Others were rotten to begin with. (It seems that the Lugano branch of Crédit Suisse was drawn into co-financing the operations of the Sindona group, which went bankrupt.) When the Italian government decided to accord fiscal amnesty to capitalists who had deposited their funds abroad, provided these funds were rapidly repatriated, the entire operation collapsed. The losses incurred by Crédit Suisse were valued at $400 million.[33]

Stress is often laid on the advantages the system of floating exchange rates offers American imperialism. These advantages, which are obvious as far as the export of commodities is con-

[32] The British and American banks, which had lost ground in their competition with Swiss banks in London Euro-dollar markets, evinced a good deal of *Schadenfreude* at the misadventures of Crédit Suisse. They even spoke of 'dangers' to the Swiss franc. This was both lacking in foundation and irrational from the standpoint of their own interests. Because of the immense volume of capital which has found refuge in Switzerland – there is talk of $100 thousand million – any bank panic in that country would automatically turn into a collapse of the international credit system.

[33] A real can of worms was uncovered in the course of an inquiry into the bankruptcy of the Italian Sindona group. The nationalized Banco di Roma had a blacklist of 500 big depositors who had fraudulently transferred 34 thousand million lire (more than $400 million) abroad. When called upon to turn this list over to the judicial authorities, the bank announced that the list had been lost (*Neue Zürcher Zeitung*, 18 and 23 November 1977).

cerned, are, however, partially neutralized by disadvantages in the international movement of capital, as we have already indicated. A continuous fall of the dollar, however, must inevitably entail disturbing consequences for international trade. In the long run, no extra-economic constraint can compel private owners to accept continuously devalued money for their commodities and promissory notes. A growing portion of world trade will thus tend to be conducted in currencies other than the dollar. Inasmuch as none of these currencies is strong enough to serve as international reserve money alongside the dollar – only a unified European currency could conceivably play such a role – international monetary disorder is inevitably aggravated.

That situation could change, however, if the disappearance of France's, Italy's and Britain's balance of payments deficits were to be followed by a new and sharp reduction in the exchange rate of their currencies with respect to the Deutschmark, designed to cheapen their exports and so to conquer new markets in West Germany. In that case, the German government could be tempted to re-open the road towards European monetary union in order to defend the commercial interests of its capitalists, which would be jeopardized much more by a decline of the French franc or the lira than by a decline of the dollar.

Hence, the dream of a demonetarization of gold remains a technocrats' utopia, despite the Jamaica accords. More than ever, gold will remain the basis of the reserves of the central banks and the 'ultimate' storehouse of value, to the very extent that the dollar, the paper-money reserve, is less and less 'as good as gold', i.e. the more the dollar loses its buying power.[34]

[34] The 'decline' in the share of gold in the exchange reserves of the central banks mentioned in the report of the Bank for International Settlements simply reflected the fact that these banks (except in the case of France, Italy, Australia and South Africa) continue to evaluate their gold reserves either at the fictitious price of $42.20 an ounce or in their equivalent in Special Drawing Rights. Hence, at the end of 1976 gold on hand represented only 16% of total international liquidity, compared with 24% at the end of 1973. But if all the central banks counted their gold according to the current price of $160 an ounce, the situation would change completely. Gold on hand would then represent more than 35% of international liquidity.

Indeed, when they talk among themselves, monetary experts use a language quite different from the one they use in public. Tom de Vries, one of the major leaders of the International Monetary Fund, wrote unabashedly in regard to the Jamaica accords: 'The preceding means that the prospects for gold during the next few years are uncertain. This uncertainty about such an important element of the system once again underscores the interim character of the Jamaica accords; they do not introduce a new monetary system in the concrete sense.'[35]

It could not be put any better. No new international monetary system for the international capitalist economy has emerged since the collapse of the Bretton Woods system. And the long depressive phase we have now entered renders the creation of such a system all the more difficult.

[35] *Finances et Développement*, IMF quarterly review, vol. 13, 3 September 1976.

4

The Impact on the International Economy: Capitalist and 'Socialist'

1. The Stagnation of the Common Market

All the projects for the consolidation and extension of the Common Market were hit full force by the recession. The nine members of the EEC were compelled to shelve the Werner plan for the staged realization of economic and monetary union, which had been decided on in 1972. The reason is obvious: the disparate evolution of the economic, monetary, and social situation in West Germany (and secondarily the Benelux countries) on the one hand and in Britain, France, and Italy on the other. Most important were the varying rates of inflation and the completely divergent evolution of the balance of payments (West Germany showed a big surplus, while Italy, France, and Britain had high deficits, at least until the last months of 1977).

Abandoning all hope of achieving monetary union in the foreseeable future, the European bourgeoisies fell back on the monetary 'snake' (that is, on common fluctuations of currencies within narrow limits). But when France was compelled to withdraw because of persistent balance of payments deficits, the snake was reduced in practice to the deutschmark and its satellite currencies.

This division of the Common Market into 'solid' and 'unstable' sectors was openly proclaimed by Willy Brandt in a speech that caused a sensation. It was then subjected to a kind of institutionalization by the Tindemans project of a 'progression' of the EEC.[1] This project amounted to proposing steps towards economic and monetary integration only among the five so-called stable countries (West Germany, the Benelux countries, and Denmark).

It could be asked whether West German big capital and the Helmut Schmidt government exhibited a lack of audacity on this occasion. Could not the acute foreign exchange crisis of Britain, Italy, and then France have provided an opportunity for a decisive step towards monetary integration in exchange for pooling of the exchange reserves of the 'rich' members? There are two fundamental reasons why the West German bourgeoisie did not dare take this option. The first is the instability, from the capitalist point of view, of Britain, France, and Italy, which is not only monetary but also, and more importantly, social and political. A radical modification in the relationship of class forces, with threats of a breakthrough towards genuine socialist revolution, is not unimaginable in these three countries. It is obvious that if this came to pass the workers' governments in these countries would in no way feel bound by the commitments made by previous governments to subordinate their economic and monetary policies – in this case the social priorities clearly formulated by the majority of the labouring population – to the veto of international capitalist organs or to a 'community monetary discipline' which corresponds to the logic of the capitalist market economy and not to any 'objective economic laws' of eternal validity.

It therefore would have been stupid for the West German bourgeoisie to begin to cover an appreciable portion of the balance of payments deficits of other countries with its 'own' exchange reserves without obtaining a guarantee that there would be a *lasting* common economic and monetary policy.

In addition, the very size of the deficits accumulated by Italy, France, and Britain – and the risk that they may be further amplified by a coming recession – is such that the West German

[1] The Tindemans report, published 7 January 1976, faithfully adheres to the line of Willy Brandt's Paris speech. As the official organ of the German Social Democracy, *Vorwärts*, noted (15 January 1976), the Tindemans report could have been written by Helmut Schmidt himself.

bourgeoisie may have legitimately feared whether it was possible to soak up this deficit by using a portion of the exchange reserves of the 'rich' EEC members. It must not be forgotten that the countries with relatively more stable economies are in no way sheltered from a rapid deterioration of their own balance of payments position if their exports begin to stagnate or even decline in an atmosphere of contraction of world trade. Under these conditions, the risks of sacrificing a significant proportion of accumulated reserves in order to come to the aid of their partners were too great for the West German capitalists, for this could have meant that Germany itself would have been unable to resist the next storm.

The stagnation and crisis of the Common Market are thus not primarily the product of the inertia of political organs, lack of imagination on the part of technocrats, 'sabotage' by the British government, or a 'lack of forward-looking politicians'. They have objective causes, closely linked to the depression of the international capitalist economy and the inevitable reactions of big capital during a phase of downturn of the economic cycle.

What is striking, however, is the fact that the essential structures of the Common Market did resist the most serious crisis of the international capitalist economy since the Second World War. Although protectionism spread rapidly in world trade as a whole, it did not develop at all strongly within the Common Market itself. Contrary to what had been thought by many observers, whether of the left or the right, the EEC did not collapse as a result of the recession.

The reason for this lies essentially in the strong advance in the interpenetration of the economies of the nine member countries during the preceding fifteen years. The dissolution of the Common Market would deal a hard blow to the exports of each member country (Table 40). The blow would be literally catastrophic for the Benelux countries, which are, not surprisingly, the most fervent advocates of the consolidation of the EEC. Moreover, this interpenetration of trade is linked to – and partly a function of – a growing division of labour within the EEC among the branches of the multinational firms or firms

Table 40

Share of Exports Within the EEC Countries as % of Total Exports of All Members

	All EEC Countries	West Germany	France	Italy	Benelux	Britain
1960	28.5	29.5	29.8	29.6	47	—
1965	36.5	36.3	41.0	40.2	47	—
1970	41.6	40.1	48.8	42.9	65	—
1974	52.7	44.9	53.1	45.4	70	33.4
1975	52.0	43.6	49.2	45.0	70	32.3

Source: Winfried Wolf, op. cit., p. 166.

associated in cooperative accords. It is backed up by a trend towards the interpenetration of capital within a series of big firms themselves. This phenomenon, although it remains more modest than anticipated by the founders of the EEC, has been spectacularly confirmed in the realm of banking and finance capital.

There is thus a contradiction – a real one – between the stagnation and paralysis of the EEC in the political and monetary domain and the consolidation of the structures of commercial interpenetration. Now, contrary to what is asserted by some currents of thought that claim to be Marxist, the role of the state as supporter of the great monopolies is absolutely essential in the imperialist epoch. If the recession has demonstrated anything, it is precisely the fact that in the long run the monopolies *cannot free themselves* from the law of value or the consequences of conjunctural fluctuations. They therefore cannot escape the tendency of the falling rate of profit. Under these conditions, the role of the state as guarantor of monopolistic super-profits is vital for the monopolies. They win or lose precious trump cards in the inter-imperialist competitive struggle depending on whether the state is more or less powerful, more or less able to play this role *immediately*.

Under these conditions, the relative power of the American state and the capacity for rapid intervention of the Japanese state, which is already less powerful than the U.S. state, contrast painfully with the impotence of the pre-state structures of the EEC and the marked weakness of the West European national states. A striking example is provided by the vicissitudes of the European aeronautics industry. This industry, which employs more than 400,000 workers (as against 1 million employed by the American aeronautics industry) and which outstrips its American competitor technologically, furnished only 8% of the civilian aircraft sold on a world scale during the past ten years. The major reason for this commercial failure is that the European governments, too weak and divided, have been incapable of guaranteeing adequate outlets. It is clear that this industry is literally threatened with extinction if the situation does not change in the medium term.

Under such conditions it is not surprising that the big European employers are evincing mounting impatience with the inertia, passivity, and even paralysis of the 'pre-state' political organs of the EEC. They are threatening to take matters into their own hands, to replace public initiatives with private ones.

The most spectacular example in this regard was the decision of the West German, Dutch, and Luxembourg steel companies in the spring of 1976 to establish a European rationalization cartel excluding the French steel companies and some of the Belgian ones. The implementation of this project would have dealt a death blow to the European Coal and Steel Community, the point of departure of the EEC itself. In the end a compromise was reached. A European cartel, Eurofer, was founded, including the steel companies of all nine member countries, primarily for the purpose of opposing Japanese competition.

Nevertheless, the crisis erupted again in December 1977. Caught by the throat by what they call 'savage competition' (imports from the 'third world' and products of the famous Italian *bresciani*, sold at prices 30–50% lower than their own), the French and Benelux steel companies took the initiative this time, threatening unilaterally to impose protectionist 'safeguard' measures if the EEC did not react rapidly. It did react, imposing exorbitant customs fees leaving *Le Monde* to talk of a 'cartelization of public order'.[2]

[2] *Le Monde*, 21 December 1977. (The trend towards the formation of public cartels, and even forced cartelization, had already been evident during the

2. The World Market and International Industrial Capital

Any over-production crisis that sweeps the world market expresses fundamental imbalances and disproportions in the production and circulation of capitalist commodities and gives rise to efforts by capital to surmount these contradictions by restructuring both production and the market. The efforts to restructure production are aimed at raising the rate of profit through the following measures: elimination or absorption of the less profitable firms, or a reduction in their activity; replacement of less productive techniques by more productive ones; reduction of the fabrication of products for which demand appears to be structurally stagnating or declining, combined with an increase in the fabrication of products for which demand is structurally rising; rationalization investments through saving on raw materials, energy, labour, and the employment of fixed capital; increases in the rate of circulation of circulating capital; intensification of the labour process; and, in general, concentrated efforts to raise the rate of surplus-value on a lasting basis (i.e. the rate of exploitation of the work force). All such efforts are obviously undermined by uncertainty factors inherent in a system based on private property and competition. The efforts to restructure the world market relate both to the search for new outlets and to the redivision of old markets in conformity with the altered relationship of forces among the imperialist trusts and powers.

We have already dealt with the latest vicissitudes of inter-imperialist competition within the domestic markets of the imperialist countries themselves, which still constitute the major sector of the world market because of their relative wealth compared to other parts of the world. Let us now examine the additional modifications of the world market now under way.

(1) The OPEC countries (or at least some of them) have emerged as significant outlets for the industries of the imperialist countries, particularly those industries exporting capital

period between the two world wars. See *Marxist Economic Theory*, chapter 16, p. 496.)

goods, means of transport, and ready-made factories. Exports of the EEC countries to the countries of the Arab League rose from 6 thousand million SDRs in 1973 to 10 thousand million SDRs in 1974, 14 thousand million SDRs in 1975, and 18 thousand million SDRs in 1976. For the OPEC countries as a whole, the

Table 41

Imports of OPEC Members (in $000m.)

Source	1972	1973	1974	1975	1976
EEC	5.7	8.0	13.5	22.9	26.2
United States	2.6	3.4	6.2	9.9	11.7
Japan	1.9	2.7	5.4	8.4	9.3
Total	10.2	14.1	25.1	41.2	47.2

Source: GATT, *Le Commerce international en 1976/77.*

evolution was as shown in Table 41. Thus, the exports of the major imperialist powers to the OPEC countries nearly quintupled in the space of four years. Even though this progression covers only 50% of the increase in the value of the oil sales of the OPEC countries to these powers, it nevertheless provides an additional outlet for many imperialist trusts. Thus, a portion of the world surplus-value redistributed in the form of the oil revenues appropriated by the owning classes of the OPEC countries has been recovered by imperialist capital. Let us add that it is often forgotten that the growing flow of oil revenue into the OPEC countries has been accompanied by a growing flow of revenue from the oil companies of the OPEC countries to the imperialist countries. This latter flow increased from $3.8 thousand million in 1970 to $6 thousand million in 1972, $10 thousand million in 1973, and $26 thousand million in 1974. But the various imperialist countries have garnered varying shares of this new pie (see Table 42).

(2) A number of semi-colonial countries of East Asia have emerged as significant partners in world trade. This applies primarily to South Korea, Hong Kong, Singapore, and Taiwan,

Table 42

Exports to OPEC Members in 1975–76 (in thousands of millions of $)

	1975	1976		1975	1976
United States	10.8	12.8	Netherlands	1.4	1.7
Japan	8.4	9.4	Belgium	1.2	1.3
West Germany	6.4	8.3	Switzerland	0.8	1.2
France	4.9	4.1	Sweden	0.7	1.0
Britain	4.5	5.3	Canada	0.7	0.9
Italy	3.7	4.2			

Note: The United States exports include a large amount of military material.

Source: Bank for International Settlements, *46e Rapport Annuel*, June 1976; *Perspectives économiques de l'OCDE*, no. 21, July 1977.

and to a lesser extent Indonesia and Malaysia. Until recently Japanese imperialism was the main beneficiary of this development, garnering significant outlets and carving out advantageous fields of capital investment. American imperialism maintains important positions here, but it is clearly slipping in comparison with its Japanese competitor. This new expanding sector of world trade is still largely *terra incognita* for the European imperialists, apart from the traditional positions of British imperialism in Hong Kong, Singapore, and Malaysia (although Britain too is clearly on the decline compared with its Japanese competitor).[3]

These countries have undergone a significant process of industrialization in recent years, a process curbed but not at all halted by the 1974–75 recession.[4] Hence, they are in turn beginning to export industrial products and even capital, in

[3] An interesting concomitant phenomenon is the appearance of a market of 'Asia-dollars' parallel to the market of 'Euro-dollars'. According to the *Far Eastern Economic Review* (17 September 1976 and 23 September 1977), this market, located essentially in Singapore, involves a volume of deposit-loans that rose from $390 million in 1970 to nearly $14 thousand million towards mid-1976 and $17 thousand million at the beginning of 1977.

[4] According to the *Far Eastern Economic Review* (21 October 1977), per capita GNP in Singapore has reached $2,500, twice the 1970 figure and four times the 1965 one. The GNP in Hong Kong was reported to be $1,700, three times the 1965 figure and 70% higher than the 1970 figure. Some 40% of the

competition with their former or present partners and backers. The East Asian industries of electrical appliances and watch-making, for example, represent serious competition for Japan-ese industry, not to mention that of the United States. South Korean entrepreneurs have underbid Japanese, European, and American entrepreneurs for more than $1.5 thousand million worth of construction contracts (for roads, official buildings, shipyards, etc.) in the Middle East, especially Saudi Arabia, taking advantage of their ability to supply abundant cheap labour. The textile industry in Southeast Asia has seriously challenged the European textile industry.

Precisely because of the relative success of industrialization in these countries, they now form a supplementary outlet for some industrial branches of the imperialist countries, primarily those branches exporting capital and transport goods. There has thus been a certain modification of the international division of labour, some industries – especially textiles, electrical appliance assembly, or simple electronics involving products of relatively high labour intensity – shifting to the less developed countries, the centre of gravity of industry in the imperialist countries shifting increasingly towards the sector of capital goods and transport goods.

But this new international division of labour inevitably means that some of the successes of industrialization in the countries of East Asia threaten important sectors of industry in the imperialist countries. Taiwan has become the world's fourth-largest producer of synthetic fibres, with an annual production of more than 400,000 tonnes. South Korea is striving to attain the same level in 1980–81 and to export $3.5 thousand million worth of nylon and other synthetic fibres annually. Because of the excess capacity now weighing on the synthetic fibres market, this expansion constitutes a serious threat for

---

non-independent active population in Hong Kong and 20% in Singapore are already employed in manufacturing industry. Hong Kong's exports reached $7 thousand million in 1976, exceeding those of Finland and approaching those of Norway, which have equivalent populations. They are more than double Ireland's exports and nearly four times those of Portugal, two of the poorest countries in Europe.

the West German, Italian, French, Dutch, and Belgian trusts. Some of them have had to initiate a genuine process of dis- mantlement of a portion of their installations, particularly in France.

In the long run, the textile industry in West Europe (both natural and synthetic fibres, as well as finished products) is increasingly threatened by imports from countries where wages are significantly lower. In 1969 total imports of textile products represented only 5% of total sales of such products in West Europe; by 1975 the figure had risen to 11%. Sales of imported products are rising at an annual rate of 10%, while total sales are rising at an annual rate of only 2%.

The example of the West German shoe industry strikingly illustrates the effects of the restructuration of the world market on one particular branch of industry. Production in this sector had been constantly diminishing in West Germany since 1968. It fell from 180.4 million pairs in 1969 to 151.2 million in 1972 and 113.7 million in 1975. Employment in the industry has been on the decline *for more than ten years*, since 1965. It fell from 100,000 in 1965 to 92,000 in 1969 to 77,100 in 1972 and to 55,600 in 1975, a reduction of nearly 50% in just one decade. At the same time, imports of shoes to West Germany rose from 58.1 million pairs in 1965 to 100 million pairs in 1974. *As of 1973, imports exceed domestic production.* The major exporting countries are Italy, France, Spain, and more recently Taiwan, which has already overtaken Spain.

A comparable evolution is taking shape in the production of primary petrochemicals materials. A number of Arab countries and Iran are attempting to enter this sector in a big way so as to take advantage not so much of cheap labour – wages are only a marginal element in production costs in petrochemicals, and the work force is largely atomized – as of the very low prices of raw materials and energy. These countries could now utilize their own oil as a raw material – at a price less than 5% what it costs Japan, West Europe, or North America. The European trusts have insisted that this sector already suffers from excess capacity on a world scale and fear that their share of the market may be drastically reduced if these projects come to fruition.

One can imagine the anxiety of the European and Japanese steel companies about the report presented to the May–June 1977 session of the United Nations Council for Industrial Development, held in Vienna. This report called for an augmentation of the production capacity of the 'third world' countries in chemical fertilizers from 15–20% to 40% of total world production capacity over the next twenty years. It recommended an increase in these countries' capacity for steel production from 50 million tonnes a year to 370 million. Since there is already significant excess capacity in these sectors and since world demand is no longer rising at a pace comparable to that of the fifties and sixties, the attainment of these goals (which is manifestly uncertain) would imply the dismantlement of significant portions of these branches in the imperialist countries.

(3) Alongside the countries of East Asia and some of the OPEC countries (especially Iran, Saudi Arabia, and Kuwait), some countries of Latin America – especially Brazil, Mexico, Colombia, and to a lesser extent Argentina – have continued to undergo a significant process of industrialization, which has partially altered their position in the world market. An event that occurred in December 1977 symbolizes this modification. Production of the Volkswagen 'beetle', the model which had surpassed Henry Ford's 'Model T' as the most widely sold automobile in the industry's history, was terminated in West Germany. The beetle is now imported to West Germany from Volkswagen's factory in Puebla, Mexico, and from other VW installations in Brazil. Indeed, Brazil's industrial exports are now cornering a growing share of the Latin American market and are tending to spill over to other continents.

To grasp the meaning and limits of this phenomenon (which is obviously restricted *to the most developed of the underdeveloped countries*) it must be understood as the combination of two tendencies that are simultaneously complementary and contradictory.

On the one hand, as we have already emphasized, a growing number of multinationals are shifting their production centres to countries with lower real wages and/or less inflated raw materials prices (among these countries are not only the most developed of the semi-colonial and dependent countries but also countries like Spain and some of the so-called socialist countries). The multinationals' ability to *transfer pollution* is another factor here:

'All the industrial countries should ask themselves whether it is in their interest to preserve on their territory such a large portion of the metals transformation industry. This is one of the industries that do not employ much of a work force but absorb much more energy and pollute the environment.

'The United States should consider whether it can afford the luxury of conserving on its territory so many factories making aluminium, in view of the fact that for some of these factories energy purchases account for a third of the real sales price. [The electrolysis of aluminium consumes enormous amounts of electricity – E.M.] Since electricity rates are continuing to rise, the producers of aluminium should ask themselves whether it would not be appropriate to transfer new refineries to Guinea, where bauxite exists and electricity can be produced at 15% of the sales price of the electricity furnished the aluminium industry in the United States.'[5]

On the other hand, a partially autonomous finance capital acting independent of and sometimes in outright opposition to the interests of the imperialist trusts has incontestably arisen in these dependent countries (that is, the most developed of the semi-colonial countries). When the Hong Kong financier and industrialist Wong Chong-po buys out Bulova, the second-largest watch-making trust in the United States from under the noses of the Swiss, American, and Japanese trusts through a particularly hazardous financial operation, he is acting not as the associate or agent of the imperialist multinationals, but as the representative of the autonomous finance capital that has arisen in this third world country. The same remark applies to the operations of the Indian Birla group, which employs more than 200,000 workers worldwide, when it leases a great Swiss textile factory in order to prevent it from closing down. More-

[5] *Fortune*, November 1976.

over, I have already mentioned the wide-ranging operations, beyond national frontiers, of Kuwaiti, Iranian, and Brazilian private capitalists.[6]

Among the major partially autonomous financial groups that have emerged in the dependent countries we may mention: in India, the Tata, Birla, and Dalmia groups, which are somewhat older; in Argentina the Bunge-Born and Sasetru groups (which have also existed for some time now); in Mexico the so-called Monterrey group (heavy industry) and the financial groups structured around the big banks, especially the Banco Nacional de Mexico, the Banco de Comercio, and the Banco Mexicano, which control more than one hundred companies with holdings of 20 thousand million pesos; in Brazil the Matarazzo, Banco Itahu-Português, Bradesco, and Aços Villares groups; in South Korea the Samsung, Hyundai, Ssangyong, Sankyung, Lucky Group, Dacwoo, Hanjin, Yulsan, and Hyosung groups, the last of which seems to be closely linked to Japanese groups; the Hyundai group is associated with Saudi Arabian capital (particularly in the Korea-Kuwait Banking Association); the Hanjin group has founded a commercial bank in association with the Société Générale; there seems to be a preponderant British influence (Lazard Brothers and Lloyd's Bank) in the major South Korean commercial bank, the Korea Merchant Banking Corporation; in Hong Kong, apart from the above-mentioned Wong Chong-po group, there is the Pao group, which has powerful maritime and banking interests; in Iran the major private groups are the Rezai, Barkhordar, and Khosrowshahi groups; in Saudi Arabia and Kuwait there are the Khashoggi group (holdings of nearly a thousand million dollars), the Ahmed group, the Ghaith Pharaon group, and in the United Arab Emirates the Tajir group. 'In the course of the past five years, land prices in Kuwait have risen 60% more than average prices. Many Kuwaiti merchants have acquired fortunes of $50–60 million through trade. When one adds up

[6] See 'The emergence of a new Arab and Iranian finance capital' in *Inprecor*, no. 10, 17 October 1974 and 'Encore une fois sur l'émergence d'un capital financier autonome dans plusieurs pays coloniaux' in *Critiques de l'économie politique*, no. 22, October–November 1975.

the fortune of a particular family, the total is formidable.'[7]

In certain cases the degree of real independence from foreign imperialist capital is obscure, and deeper and more subtle analysis is required. Are the major financial groups that have arisen in South Korea, the annual turnover of which exceeded $1 thousand million in 1976, really indigenous groups or mere agencies for Japanese groups, or are they indigenous associates of Japanese groups in the process of winning their autonomy? Only a concrete case-by-case analysis can answer this question.[8] But what is certain is that there is a conflict of interest in some markets. If the protectionist policies applied in the imperialist countries and the relative stagnation, even contraction, of world trade continue, a sharp slowdown must be expected in the growth of some key industrial branches in the dependent countries: 'Already last year the Hong Kong textile industry was hurt by the embargo ordered by Canada, which was closely followed by import limitation measures in Australia. The year 1977 began with new difficulties: the United States, Hong Kong's prime customer, which buys 34% of the colony's textile exports, did renew the multifibre agreement, but accepted only a very modest increase in imports. More serious, the EEC, the second market, accounting for 28% of Hong Kong's total sales, recently requested a 5–10% reduction in imports from Hong Kong in the case of six of the colony's key products.'[9] The 8% annual GNP growth Hong Kong has experienced during the past two years is thus probably finished.

(4) Taken as a whole, the semi-colonial countries continue to occupy a marginal position in the world market, for the imperialist system and their own ruling classes have been unable to lift them out of stagnation and poverty at anything approaching a satisfactory rate. The successes of the 'Brazilian model of development'[10] were based on a *super-exploitation of*

[7] *The Economist*, 10 December 1977.

[8] For the South Korean groups, see *Far Eastern Economic Review*, 23 September 1977, and *Newsweek*, 6 June 1977. For Iran, Kuwait, and Saudi Arabia, see the sources in our articles cited above.

[9] *Le Monde*, 11 November 1977.

[10] For Brazil, see especially Pierre Salama, 'Vers un nouveau modèle d'accumulation' in *Critiques de l'économie politique*, no. 16–17, April–September 1974.

the working class and an impoverishment of the poor peasantry.
Brazil therefore developed a domestic market that includes
barely one-fifth of the nation (the big and middle bourgeoisie,
the new middle classes, and the rich peasantry). This sets a
limit both on internal industrialization and on Brazil's ability
to become a growing outlet for commodities exported by the
imperialist powers.

*This is the fundamental reason why the restructuring of the
world market now under way will not be able to stimulate a new
accelerated expansion of the international capitalist economy.* At
most it can alter the relative weight of various industrial
branches within the imperialist countries, redistribute unemployment among various branches and categories of workers,
and modify the location of some relatively important production centres for certain international growth rates comparable
to those of the fifties and sixties.[11]

To take the example of the EEC countries, their exports to
Brazil, India, and Pakistan stagnated or declined throughout
1975, 1976, and 1977. These three countries, inhabited by a total
of nearly 800 million people, purchase fewer commodities from
the nine Common Market countries than does Austria alone,
with its less than 8 million inhabitants!

The fundamental reason for this incongruity cannot be over-
emphasized: more than half the world's population did not
share in the benefits of the rapid post-war expansion, nor even
in those of the slower growth of 1976–77. Such is the back-
ground to the discussion of the 'new world economic order' and
its largely fictitious and hypocritical character.[12]

In the final analysis, under-development is under-employ-
ment (both quantitative and qualitative). In 1970 Robert

[11] Folker Frobel, Jürgen Heinrichs, and Otto Kreye: *Die Neue Internationale
Arbeitsteilung – Strukturelle Arbeitslosigkeit und die Industrialisierung der
Entwicklungsländer*, Hamburg, 1977, offer a mass of information on the shift
of industries employing relatively large quantities of labour to countries in
which wages are low. But they neglect phenomena such as the strategy of
sectoral diversification of the multinationals and take too little account of the
highly varying dynamic of the various industrial branches on a world scale. It
is not the sectors that lead the way in medium- and long-term growth rates that
are moving to the 'third world', far from it.

[12] André Udry, *Inprecor*, no. 61/2, 11 November 1976.

McNamara, one of the major technocrats of international imperialism, summed up the situation in his speech to the conference of the World Bank: 'The cities of the third world are filling up and urban unemployment is rising constantly. The "marginalized", the poverty-stricken who fight for survival on the fringes of the farms and cities, may already number more than half a billion.'[13]

(5) The restructuring efforts of the great monopolist trusts themselves (whether 'multinationals' or not) are directed simultaneously at relocating certain production centres and at diversifying the range of production, reducing the relative weight of products for which demand is stagnating and augmenting that of products for which a significant rise in demand is anticipated.

For instance, the U.S. oil trusts, like Exxon (formerly Standard Oil of New Jersey), are striving to capture optimum positions in the coal and nuclear industries. They are even cautiously moving into the field of solar energy.[14] Fiat already conducts 60% of its turnover in sectors other than ordinary automobiles: tractors, road construction machinery, machine-tools, high-quality steel, etc. The U.S. Steel Corporation now realizes 43% of its current profits from products other than steel. The American company General Electric has gone into electro-nuclear energy, aeronautics, military equipment, and production of raw materials (uranium and coal in Australia). The big companies of the Japanese shipbuilding industry, which are now operating at 50% capacity and have seen their profits in this branch evaporate, are directing their capital investments to the construction and export of machinery, as well as production of ready-made factories. This is particularly the case for Mitsubishi Heavy Industries, Ishikawajima-Harima Heavy Industries, and Kawasaki Heavy Industries. The latter two companies have obtained contracts for the construction of

[13] Cited by P. Thandika Mkandawire, 'Employment Strategies in the Third World', in *Journal of Contemporary Asia*, vol. 7, no. 1, 1977.

[14] Of the largest coal companies in the United States, the second, fourth, and eighth are already controlled by oil trusts: Continental Oil, Occidental Petroleum, Ashland-Hune Oil, and Standard Oil of Ohio.

a de-salinization plant in Dubai, construction of electric power stations in Australia, construction of a paper mill in Brazil, and the establishment of a recycling complex for natural gas in Algeria. Other Japanese heavy industry groups have won a $500 million contract for construction of factories in Algeria and a $400 million contract for construction of an ammonia factory in the Soviet Union.

The Dutch multinational Philips has strongly expanded its telecommunications-telephone department in order to neutralize the effects of the stagnation of the electrical appliance sector. Philips, in association with the Swedish Ericsson company, carried off the enormous $3 thousand million contract for the modernization and expansion of the Saudi Arabian telephone system, underbidding ITT.

3. Agriculture and the Crisis
The cycle of agricultural production has been out of phase with the cycle of capitalist industrial production during past decades. These are two reasons for this. First, the incidence of natural catastrophes – droughts, floods, hurricanes, etc. – on production levels has not yet been entirely eliminated, especially outside the imperialist countries (where this factor has become negligible). Second, world grain reserves are controlled exclusively by four imperialist countries and one dependent country (the United States, Canada, Australia, France, and Argentina). The agricultural deficits of the non-capitalist countries (primarily the Soviet Union and the People's Republic of China) must be covered by this stock, which also covers the deficits of the capitalist countries. (World trade in foodstuffs between capitalist and non-capitalist countries is integrated to a qualitatively higher degree than trade in industrial products).

Thus, world production of foodstuffs hit the low point of its cycle in 1972, when the industrial cycle was still on the upswing. On the other hand, agricultural prices peaked in 1974–75, when the prices of manufactured products were stagnating and raw materials prices were collapsing. The collapse of agricultural prices occurred in 1976, when raw materials and industrial

Table 43

World Stocks and Prices of Foodstuffs

*World Grain Stocks
(except USSR and China)
in millions of tonnes*

1971–72	165
1972–73	120
1973–74	107
1974–75	107
1975–76	119
1976–77	140

Export Prices (in $ per tonne)

	Wheat	Rice	Corn	Soya	Sugar (cents/pound)
January 1972	60	131	51	125	7.90
January 1973	108	179	79	214	9.40
June 1973	106	205	102	470	9.38
January 1974	214	538	122	261	15.61
June 1974	154	596	117	228	23.51
January 1975	169	399	132	255	38.31
June 1975	126	346	118	207	13.65
January 1976	143	280	111	176	14.02
June 1976	147	242	122	230	12.99
October 1976	113	270	106	236	8.03

Source: FAO: *The State of Food and Agriculture, 1976*, Rome, 1977, pp. 9, 12.

prices were again on the rise (Table 43). Indeed, agricultural prices on the world market are determined not by average production costs but by marginal ones, those of the least fertile lands (or the least profitable agricultural investments) whose production finds buyers. This constitutes a remarkable verification of the Marxist theory of differential ground rent.[15] Thus, a reduction of world grain production of less than 3% in 1974 provoked a rise in prices of more than 250%. A 6–7% increase in production in 1976 brought about a price decline of more than 50%.

[15] See Karl Marx, *Capital*, vol. III, chapter 39.

142

These relatively small fluctuations in production and very extensive fluctuations in prices had an extremely serious consequence: in 1973–74 a genuine famine broke out in the Sahel region of Africa and in some important areas of the Indian subcontinent (especially Bangladesh and some regions of India and Pakistan). There was also a deterioration in nourishment in some Latin American countries. In all, local per capita production of foodstuffs in 1975 was 40% lower than the 1961–65 average in Equatorial Guinea, nearly 40% lower in Algeria, 15–40% lower in the Sahel, 10% lower in Ethiopia (compared to 1974), 12% lower in Sri Lanka (compared with the 1969–71 average), 8% lower in India (compared with 1973), and 15% lower in Kampuchea. In Latin America there were serious declines in Honduras (7% in 1974 compared with the 1969–71 average) and Panama (12% in 1972 and 1973 compared with the 1969–71 average), as well as Argentina, although to a lesser extent (3.5% in 1973 compared with the 1969–71 average).

Moreover, these averages have only a limited value, since they conceal the enormous differences in nutrition among the various layers of the population in the countries of the 'third world'. For instance, Susan George reported that in northeast Brazil the poorest layers of the population consume only 1,240 calories a day, while the richest gorge themselves on 4,290, a discrepancy that is concealed by the Brazilian 'average' daily caloric intake of 2,620. In the Indian state of Maharashtra the gap runs from 940 calories a day for the poorest people – it is difficult to see how they can survive at such a level! – to 3,150 for the richest.[16] What these figures reveal in all their starkness is that millions of the poorest inhabitants of the 'third world' *have been living on the edge of starvation or have literally died of hunger since the beginning of the seventies.*

This frightful recrudescence of famine in the midst of plenty and over-production (while potential worldwide capacity for the production of synthetic fertilizers and agricultural machinery is vastly under-utilized) is not a result of any 'popula-

[16] Susan George, *How the Other Half Die*, Penguin Books, 1976, pp. 40–41. Other figures taken from FAO report, op. cit., pp. 7, 13–15, 154–5.

tion explosion'. Indeed, during the fifteen years after 1962 world grain production rose more than 50%, much faster than the population of this planet. The world rate of population growth has been on the order of 1.9% a year, while grain production has risen by about 2.9% a year.

The famine of 1972–74 was in large part prepared in advance by the deliberate policy of *propping up prices through an artificial reduction of production and of the area of land under cultivation*, in accordance with the logic of the market economy. (Those who consider the agricultural planning of the exporting countries responsible for this fail to realize that these governments are simply seeking to lend a more ordered form to spontaneous market trends, that is, to the fluctuations of production consequent to fluctuations in prices and profits, independent of the constant rise in physical demand.) In order to reduce the enormous surpluses accumulated in the four major exporting countries during the sixties, the governments of these countries considerably reduced the area of land under cultivation. The Canadian government has asserted that it could increase food production 50% in five years' time. The U.S. government reduced the area of land under cultivation by 20 million hectares and paid farmers up to $3 thousand million a year in subsidies in exchange for not cultivating a portion of their fields. In all, *one-third* of the land that had been under cultivation in the four major exporting countries as of 1968 was allowed to lie fallow.

On the other hand, after the famine of 1972–74 production of wheat was increased 12% and production of soya beans 25% in the space of one year, according to the estimates of the U.S. Department of Agriculture.[17] Indeed, the entire deficit of the countries stricken by famine was only 12 million tonnes in 1972–73, while the reduction in potential wheat production in the United States alone was 20 million tonnes; average corn production in North America and Australia was 40 million tonnes higher in 1970–72 than in 1974–75, when the area under

[17] Charles-André Udry, 'Malthusianism and Famine', in *Inprecor*, no. 16–17, 16 January 1975.

cultivation was expanded again.

The merry-go-round of hunger continues to spin. The collapse of prices in 1976–77 led the U.S. Department of Agriculture to decide in August 1977 to reduce the area of land under cultivation by about 20% for products of human consumption and 12% for fodder. *Thus, a new famine is already being prepared for the end of the seventies.*

There are other major causes for the persistence of hunger in the world besides the violent fluctuations in production in the exporting countries. Some of these are:

(a) The economic consequences of the continuing penetration of capitalism into the countryside in the semi-colonial countries. This entails a mounting substitution of commercial crops for subsistence crops, thus provoking a decline in nutrition and calorie intake for the poor populations in rural areas. The most dramatic instance is in Mali, where production of foodstuffs dropped from 60,000 tonnes in 1967 to 15,000 tonnes in 1975. This was caused by an expansion of production of cotton and peanuts, even though the currency brought in by the export of these products did not even cover the cost of increased food imports.[18] At the same time, as of 1974 the average calorie intake of the Malian population fell 25% below the level regarded as necessary.[19]

(b) The consequences of growing social differentiation in the countryside of the countries of the 'third world', a combined result of the penetration of capitalism into the villages and of the structures of large landed property. Commercial crops not intended for consumption by the rural population already occupy 55% of the cultivated land area of the Philippines and more than 80% in Mauritius.[20]

In Latin America 17% of landowners control 90% of the cultivated land; in Asia 20% of the richest peasants own 60% of the arable land. This means that 33% of the rural population of Latin America control only 1% of the land. In Asia 75% of the rural population own only 4% of the land. Indeed, according to

[18] Susan George, op. cit., pp. 38–39.
[19] FAO: 'The State of Food and Agriculture 1976', pp. 117–18.
[20] Susan George, op. cit., p. 39.

the World Bank, in twenty-two under-developed countries one-third of the work force in the rural areas possess no land at all; in other words, they are landless agricultural workers unable to produce their own subsistence.[21]

The so-called green revolution has incontestably aggravated this state of affairs because of the accentuated social polarization it has provoked in the countryside in a number of 'third world' countries; and this leaves aside the negative ecological effects it threatens to have.[22] As for the increased credit such international institutions as the World Bank have placed at the disposal of agriculture in the 'third world', Ernest Feder has demonstrated that the greater part of this credit profits not the small and middle-sized farmers but the imperialist trusts engaged in agribusiness.[23]

(c) Finally, there are the consequences of bourgeois norms of distribution, in other words social inequality, which restricts consumption of foodstuffs among the poor layers of the population *regardless of the physical availability of food products*. Even in the imperialist countries, the rise of unemployment and persistent inflation have rekindled the danger of hunger on a scale not seen in quite a number of years. Official sources in the United States estimate that between 10 million and 12 million people are chronically undernourished in that country. The fate of retired persons living on miserable pensions is painful to see in countries like Britain, France, Italy, and Spain. In Andalusia, not far from the tourist paradise of Costa del Sol, the families of 300,000 seasonally unemployed agricultural workers have to make do for much of the year with a diet of dried bread and tomatoes.

The situation is manifestly even worse in the 'third world' countries. Indeed, sometimes famines result more from prob-

[21] Susan George, ibid., p. 35.

[22] Cynthia Hewitt de Alcantara, 'The Social and Economic Implications of the Large-Scale Introduction of New Varieties of Food Grains in Mexico', UNRISD, Geneva, 1974 (mimeographed). Curiously, this remarkable study has never been published in a form accessible to the broader public.

[23] Ernest Feder, 'Capitalism's Last-Ditch Effort to Save Underdeveloped Agriculture: International Agribusiness, the World Bank, and the Rural Poor', in *Journal of Contemporary Asia*, vol. 7, no. 1, 1977.

lems of distribution than from problems of physical availability of food. As a writer on the 1974 famine in Bangladesh put it: 'Despite losses of food, some 4 million tons of rice were available in Bangladesh according to current estimates – enough to feed the entire population for a third of the year. But the great majority of the population, which subsists at the poverty level when things go well and is now the victim of floods, is too poor to buy this rice.

'Functionaries in the aid services say that great quantities of rice were smuggled to neighboring India, where the price is twice that in Bangladesh. Local speculators have driven prices over 50 cents a pound, whereas the per capita income is $70 a year. . . .'[24]

Nothing illustrates the *capitalist* character of the market economy and its unjust and inhuman consequences better than this spectacle of half of humanity afflicted by hunger not because of a lack of food products, but because money demand cannot keep up with physical demand. In spite of the abundance of use values, exchange values are unavailable, sometimes even destroyed, millions of human beings thus being condemned to a sub-human existence.[25] Nearly a thousand million men and women live an existence that 'one hardly dares qualify as human', writes McNamara, the president of the World Bank. The Common Market countries accumulate 300,000 tonnes of butter, 400,000 tonnes of beef, a million tonnes of milk, and millions of litres of wine – all unsaleable – while so many families spent 'unhappy new years' in 1977. In 1973 some 250,000 tonnes of apples were destroyed in the EEC countries. Those who mock the 'permanent crisis of under-production' in the 'socialist countries' a bit too blithely would do well to recall that the crisis of over-production, with all its inhuman consequences, goes hand in hand with the capitalist market economy.

[24] Steve Raymer in the *National Geographic Magazine*, July 1975.
[25] The most cruel aspect of the undernourishment of young children is that vitamin deficiencies and the lack of animal proteins cause permanent and incurable reductions in intellectual capacity (see especially *Le Cerveau et la Faim*, a remarkable book by Dr. Elie Schneour, Paris, 1975).

4. The So-called Socialist Countries

The 1974–75 recession of the international capitalist economy confirmed the Marxist analysis of the non-capitalist character of the economy of the USSR, China, the 'people's democracies', Cuba, Vietnam, and North Korea. Whereas all the industrialized capitalist countries, without exception, were drawn into the whirlwind of the recession, not a single bureaucratized workers' state suffered an absolute decline in production or a re-emergence of massive layoffs or unemployment. On the contrary, these countries continued their growth in 1974 and 1975, sometimes even at higher rates than during preceding years (Table 44). It is sufficient to compare this table to Table 1

Table 44

Growth Rate of Industrial Production (in %)

	Average 1971–74	1974	1975	1976
USSR	7.4	8.0	7.5	4.8
East Germany	6.4	7.2	6.4	6.0
Czechoslovakia	6.7	6.3	7.0	5.5
Poland	10.7	11.4	12.3	10.7
Hungary	6.4	8.4	5.0	5.0
Yugoslavia	6.3	11.0	5.6	3.4

Source: United Nations: *Economic Survey of Europe in 1976*, New York.

(section 2) to realize that the fate of countries with planned economies differs fundamentally from that of the capitalist countries. The claim that the crisis was a world crisis in the sense that *all* countries were drawn into it, that the countries of 'state capitalism' succumbed in the same manner as the countries in which 'private capitalism' prevails, is either a flagrant untruth or a sophisticated play on words. Once again, history has confirmed that an economy based on collective ownership of the major means of production, central planning, and a state monopoly of foreign trade is qualitatively superior to a capitalist market economy in its ability to avert great cyclical fluctuations, over-production crises, and unemployment, despite the monstrous waste and imbalances caused by the bureaucratic monopoly of economic and political management and regardless of the distance that still separates them from a genuine socialist economy.

The difference between the two economic systems may be seen in particularly striking manner in the totally discordant evolution of investment in 1975 (Table 45).

Table 45

Rate of Change of Fixed Investments in 1975
(compared with preceding year) (in %)

United States	− 9.7	USSR	+ 8.2
West Germany	− 4.7	East Germany	+ 4.0
Japan	− 8.4	Czechoslovakia	+ 7.9
France	− 5.8	Poland	+14.0
Britain	− 0.5	Hungary	+12.0
Italy	−12.7	Yugoslavia	+10.0
Canada	+ 1.6	Bulgaria	+ 7.0
Spain	− 3.4	Rumania	+14.4
Belgium	− 3.2		
Netherlands	− 3.9		
Sweden	− 3.9		
Switzerland	−20.4		
Australia	− 3.3		

Source: United Nations, *Supplément à l'étude sur l'économie mondiale 1975;*
  Fluctuations et développement de l'économie mondiale, New York, 1977,
  pp. 76, 193.

But the generalized recession of 1974–75 also confirmed the erroneous, petty-bourgeois utopian character of the Stalinist thesis that the construction of socialism can be completed in a single country and that the Soviet Union (and some other countries with non-capitalist economies) has already arrived at the stage of a 'consolidated socialist system'. In reality, the bureaucratized workers' states are still in a phase of transition between capitalism and socialism. While no longer marked by *generalized commodity* production, they are still characterized by *partial* commodity production. While no longer under the *domination* of the law of value, they cannot yet completely escape the *effects* of that law. In particular this means that since they are still interlinked with the world market, the most they can do is to prevent strong fluctuations of prices and demand on this market from being repeated within their own, domestic production. The character of the prevailing relations of production in these countries, which differs socially from that of the capitalist countries, can prevent the repercussions of world market fluctuations from taking the form of a recession in production, employment, and income imported from the capitalist environment. But the repercussions remain, even though they are partial.

In the years prior to the generalized recession, the planners in the bureaucratized workers' states oriented their economies towards increased imports of technology and equipment from the imperialist countries. Total imports of machinery and equipment goods from the six major imperialist countries (the United States, West Germany, Japan, France, Britain, and Italy) rose from some $600 million in 1968 to some $1.5 thousand million in 1973. In 1971 imports from the imperialist countries amounted to one-third of total Soviet imports of equipment goods (the remainder coming from Comecon countries); by 1974 the figure had risen to one-half. Although the overall impact of these imports on the Soviet economy remains minimal – less than 0.1% of the machines used in the USSR are of Western origin – it is nonetheless significant in certain branches of industry. One-third of Soviet production of cement, refined sugar, and beer seems to be produced with imported equipment (from both the Comecon countries and the imperialist countries). And in certain branches that are important for the future growth of the Soviet economy – mining and oil prospecting equipment; excavating and road construction machinery; equipment for the chemical industry, etc. – these imports play an important and expanding role. Experts consulted by NATO estimate that 15% of the growth rate of the Soviet economy is due to the import of western machinery and technology; such imports reportedly account for an average of 1% of industrial production per year.[26]

[26] These data are taken from reports presented by several western economists at the 1976 colloquium 'Echanges de Technologie Est-Ouest', published under

One of the consequences of this mounting resort to the import of western equipment goods had already been that the USSR (and to a greater extent several other Comecon countries) was importing the inflation prevailing in the international capitalist economy. The planners in the bureaucratized workers' states had hoped gradually to absorb the rising costs of these imports by expanding their exports of goods produced by the new, imported installations. Indeed, on the eve of the recession, and more particularly in its early stages, the governments and capitalists of the imperialist countries were exhibiting mounting interest in an expansion of East-West trade, which they saw as a means of partially neutralizing the effects of the decline in demand on the combined domestic markets of all the western countries. This was in particular the meaning of the famous *Ostpolitik* of the Brandt-Schmidt governments in West Germany and of the Nixon–Kissinger 'détente' policy. Thus, exports of the imperialist countries to the 'socialist' countries did in fact rise considerably in 1974 and 1975, as is shown in the figures in Table 46.

But the growth rate of imperialist exports to the bureaucratized workers' states soon began to slacken. The share of these exports in the total trade of the imperialist countries is rising, but it remains quite modest. During the first quarter of 1976 these countries (including Yugoslavia) purchased only 5.5% of the exports of the EEC, 6% of Japanese exports, and 2.5% of U.S. exports. But the share of imperialist supplies in the total imports of the Comecon countries rose from 25% in 1970 to 33% in 1975.

The major reason for this imbalance in East-West trade is that the industrial products of the bureaucratized workers' states (with a few exceptions) are not competitive on the world market, either because of their quality, or because of their price, or because of a combination of both. Thus, there are only limited outlets for these products in the imperialist countries.

the same title by the economic affairs direction of NATO (Brussels, 1976). I have particularly drawn from the reports of Professor Podolski of Portsmouth Polytechnic, Professor Hanson of the University of Birmingham, and Professor Marshall I. Goldman of Harvard University.

Table 46

Exports of the Imperialist Countries to the So-called Socialist Countries

| | (in %) | | Value in thousands of millions of $, |
	Increase in 1974 (over 1973)	Increase in 1975 (over 1974)	1975
West Germany	48	16	7.1
Japan	101	19	4.7
France	34	64	2.9
United States	−17	48	2.9
Italy	65	32	2.4
Britain	23	24	1.5
Sweden	49	43	1.2
Canada	6	42	1.1
Belgium	70	4	0.9
Netherlands	59	17	0.9
Switzerland	43	25	0.8
Average:	42	28	Total: 26.4

Source: Bank for International Settlements, *46e Rapport Annuel*, June 1976.

When these exports are sold at extremely low prices – as is the case for some textile products and for shoes – it is a matter either of mediocre products or those whose sale gives rise to furious charges of 'dumping' on the part of the capitalist countries concerned, and this often evokes protectionist measures. But since exportable agricultural surpluses are constantly diminishing in many 'people's democracies' (some of which have even become net importers of agricultural products), there are only two possible sources from which the workers' states can derive the currency needed to finance their growing demand for western equipment goods and technology: rising exports of raw materials and ever greater credit from the imperialist countries themselves.

Hopes for a continuous expansion of East-West trade thus rest on the assumption that there will be a growing number of barter agreements exchanging raw materials of the countries of the East for western commodities. Examples are the trade of Soviet natural gas for pipelines built by West Germany; Chinese oil for Japanese steel and machinery; Soviet uranium for French industrial equipment; East German corn for West German Volkswagens.[27] But the expansion of such agreements is limited by the fact that the USSR, which is the only large supplier of raw materials in Comecon, is itself suffering a trend towards growing depletion and towards a constant rise in raw materials prices.[28] In order to increase its income in precious western currencies, the Soviet bureaucracy is beginning to ration supplies of oil products at reduced prices to its Comecon partners, especially East Germany and Czechoslovakia. It is increasing its sales at high prices on the world market, and is also compelling Comecon members to buy at prices comparable to those of Middle Eastern oil [29]

It is thus understandable that the share of imports of imperialist products financed by western credit is rising rapidly. There are varying estimates of the total debt to the imperialist countries that has been accumulated by the Comecon countries. They run from $32 thousand million in 1975 and $35 thousand million as of the first quarter of 1976 (Chase Manhattan Bank) to $40 thousand million (Institut für internationale Wirtschaftsvergleiche, Vienna) and even $48 thousand million (*The Economist*).[30] A portion of these differences probably results from the fact that some estimates calculate the gross credit total, while others add debt service charges, and

[27] *The Oriental Economist*, October 1976, described some of the major orders for the construction of factories abroad won by Japanese trusts, particularly construction projects worth $500 million in Algeria and two ammonia factories in the Soviet Union valued at $400 million. The saturation of many markets in the imperialist countries is nevertheless causing difficulty for this sort of barter arrangement. The 23 January 1978 *Business Week* reported a common meeting of representatives from Comecon and the major multinationals engaged in these agreements in order to 'regularize' the markets.

[28] Chinese oil production has expanded enormously in recent years, from 30 million tonnes in 1970 to 80 million tonnes in 1974 – and over 100m. in 1977.

[29] According to *Blick durch die Wirtschaft* (22 May 1975), the production cost of Soviet oil extracted from the Caucuses and the Urals amounts to some $3.66 a tonne (as against $0.50 in Iran, $0.75 in Saudi Arabia, and $1 in Libya). In Siberia, on the other hand, where 80% of Soviet oil reserves are located, the production cost is reported to be $9 a tonne. In 1971 the USSR still exported 20% of its oil production. Because of the growing needs of the economy and the rising motorization of society, however, this percentage is expected to drop sharply in coming years.

[30] 30 March 1977.

still others include the deposits (also rising) which the banks of the so-called socialist countries have placed in the imperialist countries; in other words, they calculate the net debt. Table 47 probably presents the most nearly correct approximation of the evolution of the debt of the so-called socialist countries to the imperialist countries.

Table 47

Evolution of Gross Foreign Debt of the Countries of Eastern Europe, 1973–76 (in thousands of millions of $)

	1973	1974	1975	1976
Bulgaria	1.5	1.7	2.4	2.8
Czechoslovakia	0.9	1.1	1.5	2.1
East Germany	2.8	3.6	4.9	6.0
Hungary	2.0	2.3	3.2	3.3
Poland	2.5	4.9	7.0	10.8
Rumania	2.1	2.4	2.8	2.8
USSR	4.0	5.9	11.4	16.0
Comecon institutions	1.8	2.1	2.8	3.5
Total:	17.6	4.0	36.8	47.3
Holdings in western banks	3.7	5.1	6.3	7.6

Sources: Chase Manhattan Bank, Bank for International Settlements, *Business Week*, 7 March 1977.

In general, the banking system (and governments) of the imperialist countries are not overly concerned about this increase in the indebtedness of the countries of the East. The latter are considered good risks, the USSR especially so, because of its high gold supply.[31] Nevertheless, in 1977 current charges on the debt already amounted to more than 25% of the annual strong currency income of the USSR, Poland, and East Germany and 20% on the average for the rest of the Comecon

[31] Since 1975 the USSR has raised the price of the oil it sells to its Comecon partners. But this price remains largely below the world market price, since it is calculated each year on the basis of average current world market prices over the preceding five years. It is now said to be twice the pre-October 1973 level (as against a fourfold increase for the capitalist countries). (*Neue Zürcher Zeitung*, 24 October 1977.)

154

countries. Table 48 indicates that the relation between their exports to the imperialist countries and their total debt to these countries is beginning to deteriorate in a manner that is serious for the bureaucratized workers' states, and especially for Bulgaria and Poland.

Table 48

Debts and Exports of Comecon Countries as of 31 December 1976
(in thousands of millions of dollars)

	Net foreign debt	Exports to OECD countries	Debt as % of these exports
Bulgaria	2.4	0.5	480
Czechoslovakia	1.7	1.6	106
East Germany	5.4	2.7	200
Poland	10.2	3.2	319
Rumania	2.5	2.2	114
Hungary	2.4	1.6	150
USSR	12.3	10.5	117

Sources: Chase Manhattan Bank; Bank for International Settlements; OECD; *Foreign Trade Statistics; Business Week*, 7 March 1977; *Neue Zürcher Zeitung*, 11 November 1977, mentions a debt of $42 thousand million.

Although one so-called socialist state, North Korea,[32] has had to request a debt moratorium and has halted payments, it may be assumed that the continuing increase of the 'socialist' debt to the imperialist countries is of more concern in the East than in the West. The Vienna institute cited above calmly projects a debt of $95 thousand million by 1980 if the current trend continues, or even $115 thousand million if debt service charges are included. But the governments of the bureaucrat-

[32] The People's Republic of Korea is said to owe some $1.8 thousand million to imperialist creditors, the USSR, and China; this is a result of considerable purchases during the period 1972–75. Terms have been protested for some $30 million of loans, according to reports. Japanese banks and finance companies, to which North Korea owes $120 million (a debt which has long since fallen due), have demanded that the Japanese Ministry of Foreign Trade declare the government of the People's Republic of Korea bankrupt (*Far Eastern Economic Review*, 5 November 1976).

ized workers' states do not see it that way. They are striving to reduce the rate of increase of their western imports. Indeed, the annual growth rate of East-West trade fell from 49% in 1973 to 43% in 1974 to 12% in 1975 and to only 2.3% in 1976. During the first nine months of 1977 Soviet purchases from imperialist countries declined by 8.5%. Bulgaria, Poland, and Hungary had already reduced their imports in 1976.

This uneasiness on the part of the governments of the bureaucratized workers' states probably stems from two considerations. First, there is fear that the imperialist powers are seeking to exploit this growing debt – and the rising service charges on the debt – to apply political pressure. That this fear is not entirely groundless becomes clear in the statement of Sonnenfeld, Kissinger's former assistant, who told a NATO seminar devoted precisely to this subject:

'Given that it is the East which is seeking to enter, or re-enter, the international economic system (by taking advantage of the credit offered by that system), it must, in general, accept the standard disciplines and practices of this system, even if that requires some internal changes.'[33] Earlier, Professor Peter Wiles, addressing a NATO colloquium, had argued for the maintenance (or the establishment) of an embargo on the export of advanced western technology to the countries of the East, the obvious aim being to exert political pressure.

Second, excessive debt – and excessive dependence on imports from imperialist countries and sales on western markets – introduces a de-stabilizing factor into planning and is not easily assimilated by the bureaucratized central planning system as it functions in the so-called socialist countries.

Obviously, this does not mean that the ruling bureaucracies in these countries will not strive to obtain 'strong currencies' by any possible means, so long as the debt to the West remains what it is. Among these means are some practices that irritate the working class, such as stores in which any western product (even automobiles) can be purchased, without waiting in line and without signing a waiting list, but only in exchange for

---

[33] *Nouvelles Atlantiques*, 25 May 1977.

strong foreign currency. These stores have become common particularly in East Germany, Poland, and Czechoslovakia. In Rumania the regime offers workers in the export industries bonuses in foreign currencies. In 1973 Rumania introduced facilities for the establishment of mixed enterprises with western participation (particularly with an American electronics firm); Hungary followed suit in 1974 (particularly with Volvo and Siemens), and Poland in 1976 (General Motors); however, the overall scope of such operations remains quite limited.

Even more paradoxically, at the very moment that the dollar was declared no longer convertible for gold, this currency began to be used as a 'general equivalent' and 'means of payment' in settling trade deficits among Comecon countries. Since 1975 some 9% of commercial exchanges between Comecon members have been settled in dollars. And the rule has been introduced that if any member country exceeds the 'planned maximum' of its commercial debt, 10% of the supplement must be paid off in 'strong currencies'.[34]

As for China, in order to prevent growing debt to the imperialist countries (a deficit of $2 thousand million had been accumulated in four years of trade with the West) it had to restrict its purchases of equipment at the very moment that it needed growing quantities. It appears, however, that Peking is about to jettison another old dogma of the era of the cultural revolution and has already discreetly sounded out some imperialist banks in order to examine the conditions under which credit could be granted. In 1977, however, China is said to have accumulated a trade surplus of $2 thousand million.

[34] *Le Monde Diplomatique*, September 1976. A tragicomic by-product of this thirst for western currency on the part of the Soviet bureaucracy was the attempt of the Narodny Bank of Moscow to engage in the speculative expansion of credit to private companies in Southeast Asia. After winning an important position in Singapore in the financing of rubber exports and the maritime transport of rubber, the bank burned its fingers in 1975, when the international downturn hit. It had accorded enormous credit to Imperial Securities International and to the Mosbert group in Hong Kong, which had to halt payment in September 1976. A 'socialist' victim of the capitalist recession (see *Le Monde*, 5–6 December 1977).

5. The International Economic Situation at the End of 1977

The situation of the international capitalist economy deteriorated visibly during the second half of 1977. Economic activity slackened everywhere, while unemployment worsened in nearly all countries (Tables 49 and 50).

Table 49

Evolution of Industrial Production

	1976	First semester 1977 [a]	November 1977 compared to November 1976
United States	+ 10.2	+ 6.2	+ 5.0
Japan	+ 13.6	+ 3.8	+ 2.5
West Germany	+ 7.3	+ 4.0	+ 2.0
France	+ 8.7	+ 4.0	− 1.0
Italy	+ 12.5	+ 1.1	− 1.0
Britain	+ 1.1	0	− 1.0
Canada	+ 5.1	+ 5.4	+ 2.5
Netherlands	+ 6.8	− 3.0	− 1.1
Australia	+ 5.1	− 0.25	− 8.5

[a] Compared with preceding semester.

Source: *Perspectives économiques de l'OCDE*, No. 22, December 1977; *The Economist*, 4 February 1978.

Table 50

Evolution of Unemployment in the Imperialist Countries, in thousands (monthly averages for 1974, 1975, and 1976)

	1974	1975	1976	December 1977
United States	5,076.0	7,830.0	7,540.0	6,377.0
Japan	736.0	998.0	1,320.0	1,428.0
West Germany	582.5	1,074.2	1,060.3	1,027.0
France	497.7	839.7	933.5	1,027.0
Italy	997.2	1,106.9	1,181.7	1,558.0
Britain	614.9	977.6	1,360.0	1,428.0
Canada	525.0	707.0	780.0	912.0
Netherlands	134.9	195.3	210.0	220.0
Belgium	124.1	207.8	266.6	354.0
Australia	122.0	297.0	335.0	400.0

Sources: For the EEC: *Télégramme statistique d'Eurostat*, 16 December 1977. For the other countries: United Nations.

158

It is apparent that by the beginning of 1978 *unemployment exceeded the record level of the 1974–75 recession*, crossing the threshold of 17 million for all the imperialist countries (in Spain there were 1.2 million unemployed; there were 1 million unemployed in the other imperialist countries not listed in the table). The real unemployment figure, correcting for the omissions of government statistics, was probably well over 20 million for all the imperialist countries.

No 'new' explanation need be advanced to account for this aggravation of the situation. It falls within the framework of everything that had gone before. There was no 'investment boom' to follow up the rise in consumer spending and stimulate the upturn. Investment even began to decline in the EEC countries as of the second half of 1977 (see Graph IV).

Deflationary measures clearly halted the recovery in Britain, Italy, France, and Australia. The spread of unemployment contributed to setting a ceiling on the 'recovery through consumption'. Because of the general stagnation in purchasing power, the 'recovery through exports' could profit only certain countries at the expense of others. But the spectacular successes of Japan and West Germany, as well as the more modest successes of some dependent countries, stimulated growing protectionist reflexes and therefore led to a stagnation and even contraction of world trade, which again erects limits on the recovery. It has turned out that a massively inflationary recovery in the United States alone is insufficient to redress the situation of the international capitalist economy as a whole.

An immediate plunge back into recession could be averted only on one condition: that Japan and West Germany in turn accentuate their use of monetary policy and credit policy (i.e., their budget deficits) and that the United States continue and even intensify its expansionist policy. Pressure in this direction from the United States, the trade unions, and many industrial sectors is such that it will be difficult for the Japanese and West German governments to avoid it entirely.

Moreover, the fall of the dollar itself unleashes compensatory mechanisms which significantly decrease the money supply in West Germany and Japan, if the monetary authorities in these

Graph IV
Investment in the EEC: 1975–1977

• • • • • Production of Investment Goods[1]
———— Index of Variation (16 sectors of the investment goods industry)[2]
— • — • Housing construction permits[3]
———— Housing and civil engineering output[4]

%

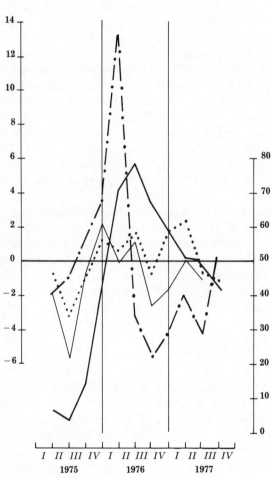

Source: EEC Commission,
La Situation économique de la Communauté, no. 4, 1977, p. 7.

countries want to avert an even more pronounced revaluation of their currencies, which would immediately imperil their exports. During the third quarter of 1977 the M_1 money supply (bank notes and demand deposits) increased 19.7% in Japan and 13.8% in West Germany (as against an average of 6.8% and 8.7% respectively during the twelve preceding months). This trend certainly intensified during the fourth quarter of 1977. It could be halted only if monetary and political authorities apply a severe deflationary policy, which appears inconceivable given the political conditions, or if they opt for massive protectionist measures and currency control measures, which would have deflationary effects on world trade.

Thus, the most likely probability is not a new generalized recession as of the beginning of 1978. On the contrary, a somewhat accelerated expansion in Japan and West Germany, combined with the expansion now under way in the United States, would improve the situation slightly in a number of other imperialist countries, because of the preponderant weight of the economies of the three major imperialist countries in the international capitalist economy as a whole. But the price that will have to be paid for such an upturn is no less obvious: intensification of the climate of international inflation throughout 1978. Combined with the aggravation of protectionist trends, this inflation will create serious financial and monetary difficulties which may compel a successive number of governments to take deflationary measures during the second half of 1978 or in the beginning of 1979. A new recession thus seems difficult to avert.

The rate of recovery in 1978, however, will be even slower, more hesitant, and more uneven by country and industrial branch than it was in 1977, despite the accentuated priming measures taken in West Germany, Japan, and probably the United States as soon as unemployment in this country worsens again. Paradoxically, the situation in 1977 was better in some dependent capitalist countries, primarily Brazil, South Korea, Hong Kong, and Iran. The recovery of industrial production after the recession was more vigorous in these countries than in the imperialist countries. GNP growth rates for Brazil were cited of the order of 8% in 1976 and 6% in 1977, for South Korea of the order of 14% in 1976 and 10% in 1977, for Hong Kong of the order of 16% in 1976 and 8% in 1977, and for Iran of the order of 12% in 1976 and 9.5% in 1977. In all these cases, however, the rate of growth began to slow as of the second year of the recovery, and a new slowdown is predicted for 1978. In addition, these predictions must take account of the consequences of protectionist measures in the imperialist countries against the 'invasion' of exports from these dependent countries; these consequences threaten to be very serious in the case of Hong Kong. The financial crisis and the crisis of over-accumulation of capital now beginning to arise in Iran should be noted.[36]

Under these conditions, the general price scales of raw materials began to slide again, although there are exceptions, tin for example. Iron and steel, copper and zinc, synthetic and natural fibres, and most basic food products, however, were on the decline during the last quarter of 1977. The price of cotton fell 33% between autumn 1976 and autumn 1977. This has had big effects on the economic situation in countries that export raw materials. Even Brazil has been hard hit by the collapse of coffee prices.[37] The inability of the oil cartel at the end of 1977 to adapt the price of oil to the fall in the buying power of the dollar and the rise in the price index for the manufactured products (especially capital goods) imported by the OPEC countries reflects the same phenomenon. In the long run, neither cartels nor private monopolies nor the concerted action of governments can prevent the law of value from asserting itself, so long as the economy of a given country remains integrated into the international capitalist market economy.

[35] *Far Eastern Economic Review*, 23 September 1977; 2 February 1978.

[36] According to the 5 February 1978 London *Sunday Times*, Kuwait averted a collapse of its infant stock exchange in January 1978 only because the government bought $186 million worth of stock.

[37] At the end of 1977 Brazil vainly attempted to counter the sharp decline in coffee prices, which followed the enormous increases of 1976 and 1977, provoked by poor harvests caused by frosts. The price collapsed from $3.20 a pound to $1.80 a pound. Brazil abandoned the old price in December 1977 (*Business Week*, 28 December 1977).

This fall in the prices of raw materials, combined with the protectionist measures taken by the EEC and the other imperialist countries, reduces the rate of expansion in all the 'third world' countries, undermines their ability to provide additional markets for imperialist production, and aggravates the effects of their indebtedness; it thus accentuates internal trends towards both a slackening of the recovery and stagnation, as well as the hesitation of capital to vigorously step up productive investment.

It is in this general context that the sharp intensification of the crisis of the dollar assumes a particular and highly disquieting significance for the international bourgeoisie. The fundamental cause of the 'free fall' of the dollar relative to the 'strong currencies' (especially the deutschmark, the yen, and the Swiss franc) lies not in the fact that the U.S. government seeks by all available means to stimulate American exports, using its 'benign neglect' of the dollar's exchange rate as a weapon in a commercial war. This factor is incontestable, but it is merely a by-product and not a basic economic mechanism. The fundamental causes of the fall of the dollar are twofold. First, the inflation rate in the United States is much higher (double or triple the current rate in West Germany and Switzerland and far above the rate that prevailed in Japan for a brief period). The second, and even more important factor is the American balance of payments deficit, which is caused not only by an 'excess of demand' (inflation), but also by a 'less competitive supply' due primarily to the ceaselessly growing gap between the productivity and efficiency of American industry on the one hand and West German and Japanese industry on the other. We have already mentioned the major indices of this gap. In spite of the rise in the value of the deutschmark and the yen relative to the dollar, and in spite of an equivalent or superior rate of increase in nominal wages, labour unit-production costs are rising less rapidly in West Germany and Japan than in the United States, because of the greater rate of increase in the productivity of labour (Table 51).

But the enormous U.S. trade deficit, which results fundamentally from the interaction of these two factors, fuels

Table 51
*Rate of Increase of Hourly Wages and of Unit Labour Costs in
Manufacturing Industries (in %)*

	Hourly wages		Unit labour costs	
	1st quarter 1976–1st quarter 1977	*2nd quarter 1976–2nd quarter 1977*	*1st quarter 1976–2nd quarter 1977*	*1st quarter 1976–2nd quarter 1977*
United States	8.2	8.7	5.9	6.4
Japan	11.1	11.3	0.7	4.6
West Germany	7.6	7.7	2.7	3.8

Source: *Perspectives économiques de l'OCDE*, no. 22, December 1977, pp.
56–57.

universal inflation through the expansion of international
liquidity. In this manner, sooner or later not only private
capitalists but even governments will be increasingly disin-
clined to be paid in vastly devalued money.

The result is a third variety of threat of collapse of the
international banking and credit system: not only the threat of
a bank panic caused by the insolvency of major credit institutions (resulting from spectacular bankruptcies in other sectors); not only the threat of the insolvency of a number of
dependent capitalist countries, which obviously sharpens the
threat of the collapse of several big banks; but also the threat
of a sharp and massive withdrawal of 'petrodollars' and other
state holdings from the American banking system and the
demand that American oil purchases be paid for in gold or
strong currencies (as well as that accounts with other countries also be settled in these currencies).[38] Central banks are
already discreetly replacing a growing portion of their dollar
reserves with reserves in other currencies (primarily the
deutschmark, the Swiss franc, and the Dutch guilder). The
share of these 'other currencies' in the total exchange reserves

[38] The report of the Church commission (op. cit., pp. 38, 39, 40) clearly
expresses fears in this regard. The precedent of the United Arab Emirates,
which in spite of their military and political dependence on Britain wound up
withdrawing a good part of the funds they had deposited there, augurs ill for
the United States. Let us note that according to *Business Week* (26 December
1977), 'petrodollars' ceased to be created as of the middle of 1977, the OPEC
countries placing their new surpluses exclusively in 'Euro-currencies'.

of all central banks rose from 7.5% in 1970 to nearly 20% in 1976, according to the International Monetary Fund. It must be very close to 25% by now.

Granted, the politico-military weight of American imperialism would be thrown into the balance to prevent such a catastrophe, and the politico-military dependence of the possessing classes of the key OPEC countries on American imperialism would be a countervailing factor too. In the long run, however, the politico-military factors will be unable to neutralize the effects of economic laws. Pressures to 'rectify' the situation of the dollar will intensify. And the 'rectification' of the dollar will require deflationary measures in the United States, which will inevitably precipitate a new, serious generalized recession of the international capitalist economy.

5

Marxism and the Crisis

1. Over-Production Crises: the Marxist Explanation

The Marxist theory of the industrial cycle, like the academic theory, has suffered from the penchant of influential authors to advance monocausal explanations for periodic over-production crises. Two great 'schools' have arisen. One claims that the crises are caused by the under-consumption of the masses (i.e., over-production of consumer goods), the other that they are caused by over-accumulation (i.e., the insufficiency of profit to continue expansion in the production of producer goods). This debate is but a variant of the old debate between those who explained the crises by 'insufficient aggregate demand' and those who explained them by 'disproportionality'.

Both schools have made undeniable contributions to a deeper understanding of crises. But they both commit the error of arbitrarily dividing what is organically linked in the very heart of capitalist production. This is the origin of their inability to elaborate a comprehensively satisfactory Marxist theory of crises, beginning from the hints Marx left us in his major works.[1] This division is particularly astonishing since Marx himself explicitly stressed in his last writings – the manuscript of the third volume of *Capital* – that the explanation of the phenomenon of periodic crises must *combine* the problems resulting from the fall of the rate of profit with those of the realization of surplus-value: 'The conditions of direct exploita-

---

[1] Especially chapter 17 of *Theories of Surplus Value*, chapters 15 and 30 of volume III of *Capital*, chapters 16, 20, and 21 of volume II of *Capital*, and the passage on crises in Engels's *Anti-Dühring*, which was at least reviewed and corrected, if not actually drafted, by Marx himself.

tion and those of realizing it are not identical. . . . The first are only limited by the productive power of society, the latter by the proportional relation of the various branches of production and the consumer power of society.'[2]

The capitalist mode of production is *both* generalized commodity production and production for profit by firms operating independently of one another. It cannot be one without the other. It is both a system oriented towards the production of a growing mass of surplus-value (of surplus-labour) and a system in which the real appropriation of this surplus-value is dependent on the possibility of actually selling commodities, which contain this surplus-value, at their production prices (returning the average rate of profit) or at prices permitting the realization of super-profits. Any other interpretation of the capitalist mode of production dispels one of the intrinsic structural characteristics without which it would no longer be capitalist.

Formulae such as the following are especially mystifying: 'Capital appropriates more and more surplus-value because it is in capital's very nature to expand in value.' Such a formulation conjures away the conditions that limit realization of the expansive tendency of capital, i.e. the contradictions of the system. (It may be added in passing that it is also sadly tautological, of the same order as the assertion that opium is a sedative because of its soporific properties.)

The very nature of the 'basic cell' of capitalist production – the commodity – implies its necessary cleavage into 'commodity' and 'money'. The commodity is *simultaneously* the product of private and social labour. But this social labour, realized in the form of private production, cannot be recognized immediately and a priori as such. The commodity thus cannot present itself immediately as social labour; it requires conditions under which this representation becomes external to it, in the form of exchange value, in the form of money. But this a posteriori recognition of the social labour contained in the

[2] *Capital*, vol. 3, p. 244.

commodity is always problematical; it always depends on the actual sale of the commodity and on the price at which it is sold.

It matters little to the capitalist that a growing mass of surplus-value has been *produced* in the course of production if he obtains only a fraction of the counter-value of this surplus-value in the course of circulation. Production of surplus-value does not automatically entail its realization. Thus, in the very division of the commodity itself into commodity and money, which is necessary if the exchange value of the commodity is to be realized, and in the contradiction between the use-value and the exchange-value of this commodity, we find the initial possibility of over-production crises.

Unlike pre-capitalist crises (or post-capitalist crises, for that matter), which are nearly always crises of physical shortage, i.e. crises of *under-production of use-values*, capitalist crises are crises of *over-production of exchange values*. It is not because there are too few products that economic life is upset. It is because it is impossible to sell commodities at prices guaranteeing the average rate of profit – that is, because there are 'too many commodities' – that economic life is disorganized, factories close, employers dismiss workers, and production, incomes, sales, investment, and employment decline.

What are the causes of capitalist economic crises? The 'over-accumulation of capital'? Undoubtedly; in a moment we shall explain exactly what this means. But not in the mechanistic sense that if only wages had been lower and profits higher accumulation, and therefore growth, could have continued unhindered. For the 'over-accumulation of capital' is accompanied by an 'over-production of commodities', and lower wage levels certainly would not have prevented that! Indeed, Marx himself derided those who admitted that there was 'over-production of capital' while denying 'over-production of commodities'.[3]

What about the 'under-consumption of the masses' (of society as a whole)? Undoubtedly this plays a role. On several occasions Marx emphasized that 'the ultimate reason for all real crises

[3] *Theories of Surplus Value*, op. cit., Vol. II, pp. 496–99.

always remains the poverty and restricted consumption of the masses, as opposed to the drive of capitalist production to develop the productive forces as though the absolute [physical – E.M.] consuming power of society constituted their limit'. This should not be understood, however, in the vulgar sense that crises could be avoided if wages were raised. For, it must be repeated, the capitalists have no interest in simply selling commodities. They are interested in selling them at *sufficient profits*. Now, any increase in wages beyond a certain threshold must inevitably reduce first the rate and then even the mass of profits and thus impede the accumulation of capital and new profits.

What about the 'anarchy of production' and 'disproportionality' among various branches of production, rooted in private property and the generalized market economy? Again, this undoubtedly plays a role. Provided one does not present a 'harmonicist' vision of this explanation by claiming that a 'general cartel to regularize production' in all sectors would suffice to eliminate over-production crises. For under the capitalist mode of production, the disproportion between production and consumption by the 'ultimate consumers' is itself an *autonomous constituent element* of the system, side by side with the anarchy of capitalist production.

What about the 'falling rate of profit'? Once again, undoubtedly this is a factor, but not in the mechanistic sense of the term, which would imply a linear causal chain of the type: fall in the rate of profit – reduction of investment – reduction of employment – reduction of incomes – overproduction crisis'. Generally, there is an increase and not a reduction in investment on the eve of a crash, just as generally there is an increase and not a reduction in wages during the period of feverish activity that precedes the outbreak of the crisis. (Obviously, there are some exceptions to this rule. In West Germany investment did indeed begin to decline before the outbreak of the 1974–75 recession.)

To understand the real sequence linking the fall in the rate of profit, the over-production crisis, and the outbreak of the crisis, we must distinguish the phenomena of appearance of the crisis, the *detonators* of the crisis, their deeper *cause*, and their function in the framework of the intrinsic logic of the capitalist mode of production.

The capitalist economic crisis is always a crisis of over-production of commodities. This is neither a mere appearance nor the product of a 'deformed ideological view'. The over-production crisis is a tangible reality which Marxism seeks to explain and not to drown in a sea of pseudo-theoretical verbiage.

Over-production always means that capitalism has produced more commodities than can be bought by available purchasing power if they are sold at their production prices, at prices that render the owners of these commodities the anticipated rate of profit. Whatever the deeper meanderings of the analysis, the first phenomenon that must be grasped is this sharp break in the unstable equilibrium between the supply and demand of commodities that prevails in 'normal times'.

Suddenly, the supply exceeds soluble demand to the point that it provokes a massive decline in orders and a significant reduction in current production. It is this sales slump, deple-tion of inventories, and reduction in current production which bring on the *cumulative movement of the crisis*: reduction in employment, incomes, investment, production, etc. And this occurs in both fundamental departments of production, that of producer goods (Department I) and that of consumer goods (Department II).

It matters little whether the slump begins in one or the other of these two departments. Empirically, it may be noted that most often it begins in Department II. This was the case for the 1974–75 recession (automobiles). But this empirical fact ex-presses no particular intrinsic logic. There have been and can be over-production crises that begin simultaneously in both departments and others – less frequently – which begin in Department I, that of producer goods.

The forms in which over-production crises emerge must be distinguished from the event that precipitates them. The detonator may be a financial scandal, a sudden bank panic, the bankruptcy of a great firm, or more simply a reversal of the cycle (generalized slump) in some key sector of the world market. The detonator can even be a sudden shortage of an essential raw material (or energy); such was the case in 1866, when the crisis was triggered by a shortage of cotton resulting from the civil war in the United States. But the detonator does not *cause* the crisis. It merely precipitates it inasmuch as it triggers the cumulative movement described above. In order for it to be able to trigger this chain of events, however, a whole series of preconditions must coincide, and these in no way flow automatically from the detonator itself.

For instance, the resounding bankruptcy of a great commercial company or a big bank generally will not strangle expansion at the beginning of a boom. It will have this effect only at the end of this phase, because all the elements of the impending crisis have already come together and are merely awaiting a catalytic event to break out.

The objective function of the over-production crisis for the development of the capitalist mode of production is another concept, which also must be differentiated from that of the forms of appearance of the crisis, its detonator, and its deeper causes. The objective function of the crisis is to *constitute a mechanism though which the law of value asserts itself*, despite capitalist competition (or the action of the monopolies).

At the beginning of every industrial cycle there is rationalization, increased intensity of labour, and accentuated technical progress. (This is especially true during the epoch of the great technological revolutions which subtend the phases of accelerated capitalist expansion, such as the phase from 1940, or 1948, to the end of the sixties.) In a market economy, a pronounced rise in productivity always means a fall in the unit value of commodities. (It matters little if this is masked by a depreciation of paper money. A price calculation in gold or in hours of labour-time would rapidly reveal this fall in value.) But a period of 'over-heating' is precisely one in which the capitalist owners of commodities – especially those industrialists who have been applying the most advanced techniques – are able, with varying degrees of success, *to hold the old values in force*, which assures them copious super-profits. The slump, over-production, and sudden breakup of the balance between supply and demand is precisely the mechanism that triggers the fall in prices. In other words, it imposes the new values of commodities that result from the rise in productivity, thus provoking heavy profit losses and a heavy devalorization of capital for the capitalists.[4]

It may likewise be noted that the upturn and the beginning of the boom are precisely the phases of the cycle in which the massive renovation of fixed capital occurs in a manner rather concentrated in time, not staggered more or less proportionally over the years of its 'moral' duration. The cyclical movement is clearly thus stimulated, and tends to be reproduced through echo effects.[5] But since the periodicity of this renovation is not strictly predetermined, since it is itself a function of the conditions of profitability, the forecasts of market expansion, and the rate of more long-term technical innovation, it is more the result of conjunctural fluctuations than their source, even though it incontestably amplifies them and contributes to reproducing them on a regular basis.

All the preceding does not constitute an *explanation* of the crisis. We have said again and again that the crisis is a manifestation of the fall in the average rate of profit and that it also reveals an over-production of commodities. We still have to establish a more exact causal chain, incorporating a whole series of indispensable mediating factors which are located *both* in the sphere of production and in the sphere of the circulation of commodities, both in the sphere of competition

[4] Inability to grasp this concatenation constitutes the fundamental weakness of the otherwise remarkable study by Makato Itoh, 'The Formation of Marx's Theory of Crisis', in *Bulletin of the Conference of Socialist Economists*, vol. 4, no. 1, February 1975. The author remains a prisoner of an imaginary dichotomy: either a theory of over-accumulation or a theory of over-production.

[4] Marx, *Capital*, vol. III, p. 250.

[5] The more rapid turnover of fixed capital, which I mentioned in *Late Capitalism*, was strikingly confirmed by a study of the Planning Bureau of the Netherlands, which reported that the age of the oldest machinery in use dropped from 45 years in 1959 to 17 years in 1973. It also reported, although too mechanically and one-sidedly, that the relative rise in wages was stimulating an increasingly 'young' investment of fixed capital, which tends to reduce employment (H. den Hartog and H. S. Tjan, 'Investeringen, lonen, prijzen en arbeidsplaatsen – Een jaargangmodel met vaste coefficienten voor Nederland', Central Planning Bureau, The Hague, Occasional Papers, no. 2, 1974).

and in that of the class struggle.[6]

At a certain point in the recovery, or in the upswing of the cycle, there is an inevitable increase in the organic composition of capital as a result of technological progress (which under the capitalist system is never 'neutral' but always essentially 'labour-saving', substituting machines for manual labour) and the swelling of investment that fuels the boom. For a certain period, this rise in the organic composition of capital can leave the rate of profit intact (this is the 'honeymoon phase' of the boom), when it is accompanied by a strong increase in the rate of surplus-value, a relative decline in raw materials prices, and/or higher capital investment in the branches or countries where the organic composition of capital is lower.

But the very logic of the expansion undermines the conditions of this 'honeymoon'. The more the expansion accelerates, the more the industrial reserve army shrinks and the more difficult it becomes to increase the rate of surplus-value, because the relationship of forces on the labour market shifts in favour of the sellers of labour-power, provided they are well organized. The longer the period of expansion lasts, the more difficult it becomes to maintain the relative decline of raw materials prices, because of the less elastic conditions of production in this sector (which is more dependent on natural factors). The longer and deeper the expansion, the more rare become the sectors (and countries) in which productive capital can find conditions of organic composition of capital structurally lower than in the essential sectors of the most industrially advanced countries.

Once a certain threshold has been reached, the totality of this inherent logic of the expansion provokes a trend towards a decline in the rate of profit. But neither prices nor production is automatically, uniformly, and immediately adapted to these worsened conditions for the valorization of capital (an adaptation that could 'mitigate' the cycle and avert a resounding crash).

[6] '... the real crisis can be represented only on the basis of the real movement of capitalist production, competition, and credit' (Marx, *Theories of Surplus Value*, MEW, vol. 26/2, p. 509).

The fall in the rate of profit accentuates competition among capitalists. Now, the technologically strongest firms and those with the greatest amount of operating capital command obvious advantages in this competition over the poorer or more backward firms. Since the former dominate the market, especially under conditions of monopoly capitalism, they seek to hold off the 'moment of truth' as long as possible – in other words, to maintain the old profit rate, and even the superprofits they enjoyed at the peak of the boom, for as long as possible.

The fall in the rate of profit simply means that *relative to social capital as a whole*, the total surplus-value produced is no longer sufficient to maintain the old rate of profit. It does not necessarily mean that the major industrial firms or the major banks immediately experience a fall in profit rates. The decline first appears in the following form: a fraction of *newly accumulated* capital can no longer be invested productively at the 'normally anticipated' conditions of profitability. This capital is then increasingly directed to speculation, risky activity which is less profitable.[7] The absolute volume of investment does not necessarily decline on this account. It can even increase. Neither do employment and the wage bill decline. They even stand at a very high, even maximum level. But investments, employment, and productivity (production of relative surplus-value) *no longer increase sufficiently* (i.e. in sufficient proportion) to fuel the expansion by themselves, apparently without regard to the situation of the 'ultimate consumers'. Industry is no longer 'the best customer of industry'.

Now, this point of reversal of the cycle, generally 'concealed' by the continuation of the boom, coincides with two phenomena that further undermine the foundations of expansion.

On the one hand, under conditions of continuing expansion and intensification of speculation, a fall in the average rate of profit must entail *constantly greater recourse to credit*, and therefore an aggravation of the indebtedness of companies. This intensifies their resistance to any rapid adjustment of

[7] Marx, *Capital*, vol. III, p. 246.

prices and profits, since the increased financial charges, combined with a fall in gross profits, would even more seriously reduce company profits. The credit boom is practically inevitable, since the banks strive to avert chain reaction bankruptcies, which could cause them severe losses. There is thus an imperceptible shift from a boom to an 'overheated' economy. For the time being, this further veils the forces inexorably preparing the crash.

On the other hand, as the expansion, not to mention the overheating, develops, instances of excess production capacity, i.e. potential over-production, *must* inevitably appear. The two fundamental features of the expansion during its 'honeymoon' phase – the increase in the organic composition of capital and the rise of relative surplus-value (the rise of the rate of surplus-value) – must inevitably result in an increase in the *mass* of commodities produced.[8] Under the capitalist mode of production it is impossible to reduce the unit value of consumer goods (which lies at the root of the rise in relative surplus-value) without substantially augmenting the total mass of commodities. Likewise, it is impossible to increase the production of machines and raw materials (production in Department I), which lies at the root of the rise in the organic composition of capital, without in the long run substantially augmenting the production capacity of Department II, even if to a lesser degree than that of Department I. The internal contradictions of the capitalist mode of production thus have the following results during the expansion:

(a) the rise of surplus value divided by variable capital

---

[8] 'Thus, to the very extent that it [machine production] increases in scope, the mass of products must increase . . .' 'The same with the *productive force*. On the one hand, the necessary tendency of capital to raise it to the utmost, in order to increase relative *surplus time*. On the other hand, thereby decreases *necessary labour time*, hence the worker's exchange capacity. Further, as we have seen, relative *surplus value* rises much more slowly than the force of production, and moreover this proportion grows ever smaller as the magnitude reached by the productive forces is greater. *But the mass of products grows in a similar proportion* . . . But to the same degree as the mass of products grows, so grows the difficulty of realizing the labour time contained in them – because the demands made on consumption rise' (Marx, *Grundrisse*, p. 422).

cannot neutralize the rise of constant capital divided by variable capital as a function of the class struggle;

(b) in spite of the spread of 'roundabout ways of production', the change in constant capital divided by variable capital *cannot* be proportional to the change in the ratio of the productive capacity of means of production to the productive capacity of means of consumption, as a function of the very mechanisms of competition and technological progress.

Under these conditions, the production capacity of Department II *must* rise more rapidly than the wage bill, particularly to the extent that capital succeeds in retarding the moment at which the rise in the rate of surplus-value begins to slacken, or halts.

The more capital lies fallow, the more the increase in the *mass* of surplus-value produced retards the accumulation of capital, the more the rate of profit declines, and the greater grows the gap between the anticipated rate of profit and the rate of profit actually realized by a growing number of firms, the gap between their financial charges and their real revenues. They are therefore increasingly at the mercy of the slightest incident, which could cause bankruptcy. 'Super-abundance' of capital and 'shortage' of profits coexist and determine each other.

In order for the effects of the fall in the rate of profit to be *imposed* on all capitals, there must be a generalized slump and a fall in prices (gold prices), which entails a contraction of production in all sectors. The over-production crisis in turn *amplifies* the fall in the rate of profit. This had already occurred despite the fact that *production of surplus-value* was at a close to maximum level. With the reduction in employment and the emergence of unemployment or short working weeks, the total mass of surplus-value produced contracts, even compared with the level attained at the end of the boom and during the period of 'overheating' – despite the rising rate of exploitation of those workers still employed. (The mass of surplus-value produced had ceased to rise at the end of the boom.)

Schematically, then, it may be said that 'over-investment' provokes 'over-accumulation' which in turn brings on 'under-investment' and a massive devalorization of capital. Only if this devalorization of capital is sufficiently ample and if unemployment and the many measures of rationalization vigorously boost the rate of exploitation of the working class can the fall in the rate of profit be checked and a new cycle of increased accumulation of capital be touched off.

The economists of the French Communist Party who have worked on the crisis are handicapped by attachment to the concept of 'state monopoly capitalism', even though they have striven to combine analysis of the over-accumulation of capital with analysis of the over-production of commodities. The notion of 'state monopoly capitalism' leads them to confused and contradictory formulas such as 'excessive accumulation' or 'wasted accumulation':

'. . . a formidable waste of accumulation has been caused by the exigencies of capital accumulation on the part of monopolies which benefit from financing of the public type. This waste of accumulation of capital and the need for profits to make that capital profitable and increase it even more constitutes the essential cause of accelerated inflation. . . . And, because of its colossal excess, the accumulation of means of production no longer furnishes sufficient outlets for compensation.'

Boccara seems not to remember that capitalist production is *always* production for profit, today just as at the dawn of the capitalist mode of production, and that the notion of 'wasted accumulation' in reference to the use-value of the commodities produced by the capitalists has no meaning in the context of this mode of production. If there is 'over-accumulation' it is not fundamentally because the state has given 'too much aid' to the monopolies or because these monopolies 'badly oriented' their investments. It is fundamentally because the *totality* of the surplus-value produced does not permit a sufficient valorization of total capital (i.e. no longer guarantees the anticipated rate of profit). The manner in which this capital is shared out among various sectors is only a secondary factor which in itself cannot cause a general over-production crisis so long as the total surplus-value produced is sufficient for the valorization of total capital.

There is one very simple way of gauging to what extent the advocates of the theory that crises are caused exclusively by 'under-consumption' and the advocates of the theory that they are caused exclusively by 'over-accumulation' are both partially correct and partially mistaken. Imagine the following dialogue of the deaf between two fervent defenders of these counterposed theories (let us say a reformist trade unionist of neo-Keynesian inspiration and an employers' representative of neo-liberal inspiration): 'Since there is a sales slump, which means an over-abundance of commodities, we must immediately raise wages in order to reabsorb unsaleable inventories and prime the pump. Otherwise there is no way out of the crisis.'

'Poor misguided soul! The crisis is primarily the reduction in investment (and therefore employment) because of the fall in profits. If you increase wages at this point of the cycle, you will further cut investment and therefore employment. On the contrary, we must reduce wages immediately. Then company directors will see higher profits coming in and they will proceed to make new investments and hire new personnel, which will turn the cycle up again.'

'Never have I heard such insanity! There is already a huge sales slump. If you reduce wages you will reduce the current purchasing power of the masses, you will reduce aggregate demand. If aggregate demand is reduced the sales slump will get worse and the market will be glutted with unsaleable commodities. Has anyone ever heard of employers investing to produce even more unsaleable commodities? If you reduce wages you will worsen the crisis instead of overcoming it.'

The fundamental mistake made by both schools, a mistake which is quite similar to that made by academic schools that operate solely with macro-economic categories (the 'aggregate demand' of the Keynesians and the 'money supply' of the monetarists), is to presuppose a number of *mechanical and generalized adjustments* which actually occur only under certain precise conditions. A rise in household incomes really 'primes' the cycle only if it is accompanied by a rise in the rate of profit and a prospect of generalized expansion of the market. Otherwise investments do not follow. On the other hand, a rise in profits and investments permits the crisis to be overcome only if it is accompanied by an expansion in aggregate demand. Otherwise inventories of unsaleable commodities continue to weigh on the market and hold the economy in depression. Thus, if there is to be a new cycle of expansion in the production and accumulation of capital, there must be a *conjoint* strong expansion of the market (of the purchasing power of the ultimate consumers) and a pronounced rise in the average rate of profit. But this coincidence depends on the conjunction of many different circumstances.[9] It is impossible to produce it at any given moment through this or that government measure (or private agreement). Hence the uncontrollable character of the cycle.

One may wonder why, after 150 years of experience, the capitalists generally act all at once rather than 'compensating' their reciprocal errors in forecasting. Why do all firms augment their investments during the boom (excessively), since that is what precipitates excess capacity and over-production? Why do they all reduce their investments during the crisis, which accentuates the slump and the decline in profits? Is it some irrational 'herd instinct' that makes them behave in this manner?

The answer is simple: what is rational *from the standpoint of the system as a whole* is not rational from the standpoint of each great firm taken separately, and vice versa. When the market is in a phase of strong expansion, all firms must attempt to cut themselves a larger slice of the larger pie; they thereby precipitate 'over-investment' and excess capacity. When there is a slump, it is absurd for each individual firm to increase production capacity. On the contrary, the losses and the fall in prices (gold-prices) must be reduced, which means that production

---

[9] A typical example: Paul Mattick writes in *Marx and Keynes*, London, 1969, p. 79: 'The slump on the market must be caused by the fact that labour is not sufficiently productive to satisfy the needs of the accumulation of capital. It is because not enough has been produced that capital has been unable to expand at the rhythm necessary to fully realize [the value of] everything that has been produced.' In other words: if profits and investments had risen adequately, there would have been no slump in the sale of consumer goods. Marx held a categorically different view, as is clear from the quotations above.

must be reduced. This in turn leads to cumulative 'under-investment' at the macro-economic level.

The naïve conviction of liberals that 'the common interest' is perfectly served if each individual pursues his 'private interest' turns out to be manifestly illusory at all decisive turns in the cycle – apart from the fact that it seeks to mask the contradiction between the interests of the capitalists and the interests of the wage earners. *Private property is the insurmountable obstacle to a staggered increase in investment*. It is thus the insurmountable obstacle to the disappearance of the cycle.

There will be those who charge that our analysis of the present crisis, as well as the Marxist theory of crises sketched out here, lends excessive importance to phenomena relating to outlets, and therefore demand. We would answer that in the final analysis fluctuations in the cycle are always fluctuations in accumulation, and therefore in the expanded reproduction of capital. But the process of reproduction of capital is precisely the *unity of the processes of production and circulation*, as Marx explained in great detail in the second volume of *Capital*. To attempt to explain the phenomenon of crises exclusively by what occurs in the sphere of production (the production of a quantity of surplus-value insufficient to assure capital an acceptable rate of profit), leaving aside the phenomena of the realization of surplus-value – i.e. circulation, which means the market – is in reality to eliminate a fundamental feature of capitalist production, namely that it is *generalized commodity production*. In Marx's words:

'Over-production is specifically conditioned by the general law of the production of capital: to produce to the limit set by the productive forces, that is to say, to exploit the maximum amount of labour with the given amount of capital, without any consideration for the actual limits of the market or the needs backed by the ability to pay; and this is carried out through continuous expansion of reproduction and accumulation and therefore constant reconversion of revenue into capital, while on the other hand the mass of the producers remain tied to the average level of needs, and must remain tied to it according to the very nature of capitalist production.'[10]

[10] *Theories of Surplus Value*, vol. 11, pp. 534–35.

And even more succinctly:

'The whole dispute as to whether *over-production* is possible and necessary in capitalist production revolves around the point whether the process of the realization [valorization] of capital within production directly posits its realization in circulation; whether its realization posited in the production process is its *real* realization.'[11]

2. The Cycle of 1972–78

If we want to apply this general theory of crises to the explanation of the 1972–78 cycle, and more precisely to the origins and aftermath of the generalized recession of 1974–75, we must incorporate a whole series of particular elements that flow from the situation and from the specific contradictions of the international capitalist economy at the beginning of the seventies. This recession, as well as the hesitant recovery that followed it and lent the period 1974–78 a clearly depressive character, must be understood as a focal point of *five different crises:*

(1) *A classical over-production crisis;* limited in depth and duration by *deficit spending* and a large-scale expansion of credit, but marked by a clearly declining efficacy of these anti-crisis techniques.

The total expansion of the public and private debt in 1975 and 1976 must have been of the order of $400–500 thousand million. Loans to the weakest imperialist governments, to the monopolies hit hardest by the crisis, to the 'third world' countries, and to the so-called socialist countries *partially* took over from loans to consumers and the most solid capitalist firms. As of 1976 the latter sought primarily to use their increased profits to reduce the weight of their debts. The credit cycle has thus conserved a certain degree of autonomy from the industrial cycle, which permitted a repetition of the 1929–32 crisis to be averted once again. (This relative autonomy of the credit cycle is one of the fundamental characteristics of 'late capitalism' as

[11] *Grundrisse*, pp. 410–11.

it has been functioning for more than thirty-five years.)

(2) The combination of the classical over-production crisis with *the reversal of the 'long wave'*, which has ceased to work in an expansive direction since the end of the sixties. High 'technological profits' – the monopolistic super-profits long realized by leading branches such as automobiles, electronics, chemicals, fabrication of scientific apparatuses, etc. – are gradually declining or disappearing altogether.[12]

In a remarkable study published by the review *Futuribles* (autumn 1977) Orio Giarini noted in regard to the synthetic fibre industry: 'The cycle is reaching a certain maturity that could have been discerned back in the sixties: the new inventions cover only increasingly marginal possibilities of utilization, disappointing the hopes for a great upturn. With time, research is being concentrated primarily on the improvement of the existing apparatus. *We have obviously entered a phase of decreasing technological yields.* . . . We see . . . similar signs in other industries: in the sector of large computers . . . for IBM, what had been planned for 1976 under the FS (Future Systems) programme has been postponed seven or eight years. . . . Likewise, . . . civil aviation. . . .'

The disappearance of technological profits is thus an additional important factor in the confirmation that the rate of profit *in the long term* will remain below the average of the fifties and sixties.

(3) A new phase in the *crisis of the imperialist system*, of which the rise in oil prices and the negotiations over a 'new world economic order' are only indirect reflections. Over a quarter of a century, imperialism was led gradually to shed the colonialist system, to make the transition from direct to indirect domination of the semi-colonial and dependent countries, but without modifying (except marginally) the division of world surplus-value between the imperialist bourgeoisie and the owning classes of the semi-colonial countries. This enter-

---

[12] 'Even if only because revolutionary technical innovations are becoming rather rare, in the future the formation of fixed capital should no longer expect to attain the level of the years of expansion, even if activity picks up vigorously' (*Notices économiques* of the Union de Banques Suisses, November 1977).

prise finally ended in failure. At the beginning of the seventies, the deterioration in the worldwide relationship of forces at the expense of imperialism compelled it to grant the owning classes of OPEC a considerably larger share of world surplus-value through a sharp and enormous increase in oil profits. The exact share of world surplus-value thus redistributed is difficult to calculate. To give an idea of the order of magnitude, however, I would estimate it at some 7–8%.

(4) *An aggravated social and political crisis in the imperialist countries*. This results on the one hand from the conjunction of the economic depression and a *specific ascending cycle of workers' struggles*, a rise in the combativity and politicization of the workers in a whole series of imperialist countries, and on the other hand from the reactions provoked by the attempt of the imperialist bourgeoisie to make the workers bear the burden of the crisis and the redistribution of world surplus-value (Table 52).

(5) The conjunction of these four crises and the structural crisis of bourgeois society that has been developing under the surface for more than a decade has accentuated the *crisis of all bourgeois social relations and more particularly the crisis of capitalist relations of production*. The credibility of the capitalist system's ability to guarantee a constant improvement in living standards, employment, and the consolidation of democratic rights has been strongly undermined as a very function of the effects of the recession.

Long waves tending towards stagnation in no way imply a permanent depression of material production over a period of twenty or twenty-five years. They are characterized by a succession of over-production crises and periods of recovery and rise in production, exactly like the long waves tending towards expansion. The cycle continues to function as such. The difference is that during the long waves tending towards expansion the phases of recession are shorter and less profound, the phases of recovery and boom longer and more prosperous. On the other hand, during the long waves tending towards stagnation recessions are longer and deeper and recoveries shorter and less expansive. It is more difficult for the

Table 52

Evolution of Strike Struggles (in yearly averages)

A. *Number of strikers (in thousands)*

	United States	Japan	West Germany	Britain	France	Italy
1951–55	2,468	—	205	658	1,415	2,343
1956–60	1,710	—	68	771	1,414	1,685
1961–65	1,362	—	186	1,512	2,102	2,971
1966–70	2,653	—	111	1,393	3,755	4,044
1971	3,280	1,896	536	1,171	3,235	3,981
1972	1,714	1,544	23	1,722	2,721	4,405
1973	2,251	2,232	185	1,513	2,342	8,081
1974	2,700	8,500	250	1,601	—	8,464

B. *Number of strike days (in thousands)*

	United States	Japan	West Germany	Britain	France	Italy
1951–55	32,220	—	1,193	2,382	3,894	4,974
1956–60	32,320	—	707	4,446	1,980	5,581
1961–65	27,300	—	486	2,562	2,794	13,017
1966–70	45,166	—	157	5,540	32,138	17,676
1971	47,592	5,777	4,484	13,552	4,392	14,799
1972	23,918	3,871	66	23,909	3,912	19,497
1973	27,949	4,210	563	7,200	3,915	20,402
1974	40,505	9,684	1,051	14,740	3,380	16,747

Sources: Huffschmid/Schui: *Handbuch zur Wirtschaftskrise in der BRD 1973–1976*, Pahl-Rugenstein Verlag, Cologne, 1976, p. 39, based on various West German sources. These figures should be treated with caution; they are based on a mixture of government and trade-union statistics. Nevertheless, they do provide an indication of a clear trend.

recoveries to turn into phases of prosperity in the real sense of the word. We have just lived through a striking confirmation of this.

The long-term tendency of the average rate of profit to decline had made itself felt since the end of the sixties, even during the second half of the sixties. The appearance of excess capacity in a growing number of important industrial branches and the increasingly speculative character of the successive phases of prosperity were the most revealing sign of this. The 1972–73 boom was almost entirely speculative. Although the spectacular increase in raw materials prices during this phase also had intrinsic causes (under-equipment and excessively low growth rates in the production of raw materials during the preceding period) and represented a product of accelerated inflation throughout the international capitalist economy as a whole, there can be no doubt about its fundamentally speculative source. The total value of all future contracts in raw materials rose from $60 thousand million in 1964 to $340 thousand million in 1974. Enormous quantities of speculative capital flowed into raw materials exchanges, both to cover losses in the buying power of the dollar and other paper monies and to realize speculative profits, since a more or less lasting shortage of raw materials was anticipated.[13]

This speculative boom was condemned to collapse into a particularly serious recession since excess capacity was more widespread than at any time since the Second World War and the acceleration of inflation compelled political and monetary authorities to erect a ceiling on the policy of expansion of credit. Thus, over-production, beginning in the automobile and construction industries, assumed the cumulative movement and scope seen in 1974 and 1975. As we demonstrated above, the partial attempts to restructure the world market and increase the rate of profit were not of sufficient scope to assure a lasting, cumulative, and rapid recovery.

In other words, the new outlets in the OPEC countries, the most industrialized of the dependent countries, and the so-called socialist countries, as well as the outlets created by the heavy increase in the public debt (the budget deficits), which in the United States was combined with a strong new upswing of household debt in 1977, did not fully compensate for the losses

[13] Concerning 'speculative purchases of raw materials' during the period 1972–74, the forty-seventh annual report of the Bank for International Settlements wrote: 'At that time, cover and speculation purchases engendered by great fluctuations in exchange rates played an important role, and this movement was accelerated in some cases by the growing supply difficulties in raw materials. This situation is perfectly illustrated by the accumulation and hoarding of considerable stocks of basic products by industrialists' (*47e Rapport Annuel*, op. cit., p. 38). A graph printed in the same publication indicated that the raw materials stocks held by the transformation industries in the imperialist countries, which had risen on the average only 0.5%–0.8% per quarter between 1968 and 1971, were rising at something like 2–3% in 1972, 1973, and the beginning of 1974; in other words, the rate of growth quadrupled.

in outlets caused by massive unemployment, the more moderate recourse to credit by the big firms, the spectacular decline in mortgage credit over a two-year period, and the contraction of household debts in most of the imperialist countries. (This debt increased strongly again in the United States in 1977.)[14] There was some 'compensation' and therefore a recovery, but it was only partial and insufficient. There was a rise in the rate of profit, but not enough to fuel a real boom.

To give an idea of the difficulties an economic recovery would have to overcome to approach the average growth rates of the fifties and sixties, let us cite three sets of figures:

(1) The difference between peak pre-recession levels of inventories in key commodities for American industrialists and merchants and the lowest levels reached since the recession (June 1975) is only $10 thousand million. (The decline was from $273 thousand million to $263 thousand million.) By September 1977 inventories were already up to $327 thousand million, which, taking account of inflation, is equivalent to about $284 thousand million in 1974–75 dollars. Thus, there was some 'pruning' and 'devalorization' of capital, but it was derisory, rapidly neutralized when the recovery began. The expansion of the market remains marginal. It is not at all sufficient to induce industrialists to make significant investments.

(2) The average annual growth rate of the production capacity of manufacturing industry in West Germany was 6.1% during the period 1960–65. It declined to 3.9% for the period 1966–70. But it fell to 1.8% in 1975, 1.5% in 1976, and 1% in 1977. Such is the objective effect of the enormous excess capacity weighing on the market. The severely limited reduction in the number of firms and in potential productivity – so far generally confined to small and medium-sized companies – has scarcely altered that excess capacity substantially.

Graph V eloquently indicates the extent to which it is becoming more difficult, from recession to recession, to reab-

[14] During the first ten months of 1977 consumer credit rose 45%(!) compared with the 1975 level (*Business Week*, 16 January 1978). Once again, the (mini-) boom in automobiles in the United States in 1977 was a boom in inflation of credit.

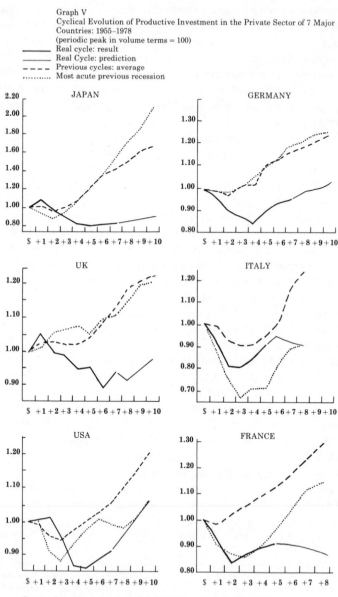

Graph V
Cyclical Evolution of Productive Investment in the Private Sector of 7 Major
Countries: 1955–1978
(periodic peak in volume terms = 100)
———— Real cycle: result
———— Real Cycle: prediction
– – – – Previous cycles: average
·········· Most acute previous recession

Source: *Perspectives économiques de l'OCDE*, no. 21, July 1977, p. 23.

sorb excess capacity. *That is the fundamental reason why there was no boom after the 1974–75 recession.*

(3) *Despite the end of the recession, the volume of 'idle' capital has continued to grow.* In mid-June 1977 the total of investments in Euro-dollars and Euro-currencies had attained $200 thousand million. At the end of 1977 it probably stood at $350 thousand million.[15] But this over-accumulation of money-capital is not unrelated to over-production and excess production capacity. 'If the United States had to invest approximately 20% of its GNP in new capacity, there would not be enough warehouses to store all the unsold merchandise, nor enough electronic calculators to make out the unemployment checks.'[16]

It may be asked why international monetary questions played an increasingly unsettling role in several of the turns in the cycle throughout the period 1972–78 (one could even say the successive cycles from 1967 to 1978, if one began from the West German recession of 1966–67 and the American mini-recession of 1967).

Because of the growing internationalization of capital, the emergence of multinational firms as the typical form of organization of large-scale capitalist production, the world market is increasingly the arena in which the real socialization of labour takes place. The value of commodities, not only that of raw materials but even that of products of manufacturing industry, tends more and more to be determined in the world market and no longer on the national markets of the capitalist countries. This means that as a result of qualitative advances in the international mobility of capital, there has been an evolution, little by little, towards *international production prices* for a growing number of commodities, that is, towards an international equalization of the rate of profit. World prices are less and less derived from national prices. On the contrary, it is the

[15] 'The Euromarket is thus increasingly becoming an extraterritorial centre of deposits for idle capital, whether short-term or long-term. . . . Today, in many great industrial countries of the western world, there are not only jobless people, but also "unemployed capital"' (*Frankfurter Allgemeine Zeitung*, 20 October 1977).

[16] *Business Week*, 16 January 1977.

price on the national market which deviates to a greater or lesser extent from the axis constituted by the world market price.

Obviously, this is a matter of a *tendency in its beginning stages*, coming to the fore gradually, and not an already widespread or even universal rule. This tendency results notably from the game of compensation played within the multinational firms, which produce simultaneously in various countries, sometimes with a significant international division of labour within the same firm for a given finished product. This product is then sold at the same price in all countries, taking account of the fluctuations in exchange rates.

Under these conditions, the monopolies are beginning to run into serious difficulties in maintaining rigid prices and monopolistic super-profits on the national markets of the imperialist countries, because of the mounting pressure of international competition. The 12 December 1977 issue of *Business Week* published a long study on the erosion of the old practices of monopoly pricing in the United States and the growing application of 'more flexible' and 'more differentiated' prices. Here again, it is a matter merely of the beginning of a turn in the trend and not at all a generalized change. Protectionism, cartelization, and centralization of firms all represent attempts, widely utilized during the present cycle, to protect monopolistic super-profits. In the longer run, however, their efficacy is dubious, because of the growing internationalization of capital and of production itself.

Under these same conditions, attempts by national bourgeois governments to 'regularize' the cycle at the national level are also meeting growing difficulties, mediated precisely by the fluctuations in the balances of payments and exchange rates of national paper monies. The transition to floating exchange rates was an attempt to bolster the independence of action of these governments in face of the imperatives of the law of value, which is increasingly asserting itself, particularly on the international capitalist market. But the results have been mediocre and ever more dubious, even for the most powerful imperialist government, that of the United States.

The more national governments manipulate the money supply, volume of credit, and artificial exchange rates on the national level, the more protectionist policies are applied and the internationalized productive forces rebel against these manipulations, the more the laws of the market – the law of value – trigger compensatory mechanisms that render these government measures ineffective or even counter-productive.

A number of governments, not only in the 'third world' but also in imperialist countries (Portugal, Italy, and Britain; and tomorrow it will probably be the turn of Spain and France), faced *diktats* from the International Monetary Fund during the 1972–78 cycle when discussions arose as to whether their balance of payments deficits, which had suddenly risen beyond the 'normal' average, could be covered by substantial international loans. Some have claimed that the personnel of the International Monetary Fund represent an ominous conspiracy of American imperialism (or of 'American–German imperialism') against the 'peoples of the world'. The reality is at once more sober and more ominous.

From a 'technical' standpoint, the representatives of the IMF, as good bankers, can grant large loans only if minimum conditions of repayment are guaranteed. Now, for the countries suffering from rising balance of payments deficits, the ability to repay loans *in foreign currency* obviously depends on increased currency holdings, i.e. the elimination of the balance of payments deficits. Depending on whether they are feeling the pressure of this or that fraction of the international bourgeoisie, these technocrats can be more or less accommodating in regard to this or that government (they were much more accommodating in regard to Pinochet than they were in regard to the Portuguese Armed Forces Movement in 1975, for example). Essentially, however, this is merely a classic confirmation of the rule that the function creates the organ. The organ *cannot* act otherwise than to carry out the mission for which and by which it was established.

Behind this technical mechanism, however, stands a socioeconomic reality which must be kept in view. The technique does not simply drop from the sky. Nor does it correspond to 'eternal economic laws'. It results from an institutional frame-work that corresponds to specific social relations and class interests. What is commonly referred to by a coy and mystify-ing euphemism as the 'open' economy is not equally open to everyone. It is an economy open to money and the owners of money. Once accumulated beyond a certain threshold this money is spontaneously and continuously transformed into capital, that is, into a potential capacity to appropriate a fraction of surplus-labour. It is able to undergo this trans-formation into capital only because the means of production are private property and there is a class of hundreds of millions of people throughout the world who have access neither to these means of production nor to the means of their own sub-sistence; they *must* therefore sell their labour-power to the owners of the machines and of agribusiness.

Since production is increasingly organized on an interna-tional scale, national borders must be 'held open' to inflows and outflows of capital as well as commodities. Because of contem-porary technique, industrial capitalism could not survive if its capital and commodities were hermetically sealed within the boundaries of small national states, any more than it could have arisen in the counties and dukedoms of the Middle Ages.

In the context of the intrinsic logic of capital, however, so long as there is no world government, world money, and world arbiter to rule in sovereign fashion over the increasingly sharp inter-imperialist conflicts and the conflicts between the im-perialist bourgeoisie and the ruling classes of the dependent and semi-colonial countries, borders can be 'held open' to inflows and outflows of money-capital only if everyone submits to certain objective 'rules of the game' which precisely permit the law of value – i.e. the logic of capital – to arbitrate these conflicts and 'resolve crises'. *The International Monetary Fund is merely the embodiment of this objective logic*, regardless of the minor liberties it may take on secondary questions, depending on which imperialist interest groups command hegemony (it is not always the same groups).[17]

[17] 'The IMF has, to a certain extent, always had a role of policing countries' balance of payments and of advising members to undertake adjustments when

We maintain that this explanation of the role of the IMF is at once more sober and more ominous than the 'conspiracy' theory. For it implies that whatever the composition of the body, and whatever the inclinations of the governments represented in it, there is no way to escape its *diktats* in the long run, unless the logic of capital is broken, along with the capitalist mode of production and all the international institutions that sustain it.

Such is the fundamental explanation of the gravity of the 1974–75 recession and the morose character of the recovery of 1976–78. Hovering over the future recession is the triple threat of a major bank crash, the insolvency of some important dependent or semi-colonial countries, and a crisis or collapse of the dollar. To this is added the threat of the overthrow of the capitalist system in one or several countries of southwest Europe, and in parts of Africa, with all the consequent repercussions for the international capitalist economy. As may be seen, the partisans and apologists of this system certainly have no grounds for optimism.

But the system is not at all at the end of its rope. It still commands significant reserves in most of the imperialist countries, enormous reserves in the richest ones (primarily but not exclusively the United States, West Germany, Switzerland, Japan, the Netherlands, Sweden, Belgium, Canada, and Australia) and substantial reserves in those imperialist countries more deeply affected by depression (primarily Britain and France, but even Italy and Spain, which are worse off). It commands substantial reserves in the richest OPEC countries,

---

they are in chronic disequilibrium. . . . An alliance [!] between the IMF and the commercial banks would be facilitated by the fact that these institutions have similar [!] views of what adjustment policies deficit countries should adopt, although their reasons may differ slightly. In the case of the IMF, it is a question of a historic institutional orientation: the Fund was created to oversee the world's monetary system, and exchange-rate stabilization is its primary responsibility. Since chronic balance of payments deficits and a high rate of inflation are the main cause of deteriorating exchange rates, the IMF naturally [!] places great emphasis on policies that will eliminate such deficits and slow domestic inflation. For the private bankers, it is a matter of self-interest: they want to make sure that the countries to whom they have lent money will earn enough foreign exchange each year to meet their loan repayments' (Report of the Church commission, op. cit., p. 63).

Brazil, Hong Kong, Singapore, and South Africa. And above all, it combines these still considerable economic reserves and resources with an arsenal of political, ideological, and military weapons to be used in the service of a cause it will pursue tenaciously for long years: a substantial new rise in the rate of profit through a sharp upturn in the rate of surplus-value.

Such an upturn is impossible without a very severe political and social defeat for the proletariat of the imperialist countries, the colonial revolution, and/or the bureaucratized workers' states during the coming decade. A defeat of this kind would not necessarily have to take the form of a victory of fascism or a victorious war of aggression against the Soviet Union, the 'people's democracies', or the People's Republic of China aimed at substantially enlarging the geographic arena of the valorization of capital – although if the defeat assumed catastrophic scope it could threaten to take these forms. It is incontestable, however, that we are approaching battles comparable to those of the thirties and the beginning of the forties, as a result of the iron logic of the accumulation of capital. The international working class enjoys much more favorable conditions today than in the past to emerge from these battles victorious. But the stakes are enormous. Because of the gravity of the crisis of the system, the accumulation of weapons of massive destruction, and the new rise of irrational and pathological tendencies towards contempt and hatred for humanity among the possessing classes and a portion of the ideologues and politicians in their service, the present crisis confronts humanity with an apocalyptic version of the alternative 'socialism or barbarism', 'survival or collective annihilation'.[18]

3. The Workers' Movement and the Crisis

Every over-production crisis always constitutes a massive attack on wage labour by capital. By increasing both unemployment and fear of unemployment, the crisis tends to force

[18] Let us mention just two extreme forms of inhumanity which have been on the rise for years: the use of 'the food weapon' (see Emma Rothschild, 'The Economics of Starvation', *International Herald Tribune*, 12 and 14 January

the workers to accept declines (or stagnation) of real wages, speed-up, the loss of previous gains in working conditions and social security, and the reduction of protection that had been erected during the phase of prosperity against the most flagrant instances of poverty and injustice.

So it has been during every crisis, and so it was during the crisis of 1974–75. Since the end of the crisis, we have seen a *universal austerity offensive of big capital against wage labour.* The probable result of this offensive will depend on the inter-action of four factors: the objective relationship of class forces; the degree of organization, combativity, and class conscious-ness of the proletariat at the moment this offensive is unleashed (which is itself a function of all that has happened during the past fifteen or twenty years of class struggle and within the workers' movement in each capitalist country taken separately and in the world as a whole); the reactions of the mass organ-izations of the workers' movement, primarily the unions, but also the traditional mass parties; the relationship of forces within the proletariat between the bureaucratic apparatuses on the one hand and the new workers' vanguard that has emerged from the struggles of the past ten years on the other hand (including an additional element, decisive in the long run: the relative strength of the new revolutionary leadership now in the process of formation).

If one were to draw a sober balance-sheet of all that has happened in the imperialist countries during the past three years, one would have to conclude that although the employers' offensive has won some more or less important successes in some countries, it has nowhere attained its goals. Workers' combativity has not been broken, nor has the workers' van-

----

1977), which even takes the form of projects deliberately to reduce the popula-tion of the 'third world' countries through starvation; and the spread of prac-tices of torture in *dozens* of countries (see the torture report of Amnesty International). For the merely 'potential' tendencies towards barbarism, note the proposals to use lobotomies (i.e. cerebral mutilation) to discipline those who 'deviate from the norm' (see especially Michel Bosquet, *Ecologie et Politique*, Paris, 1975), and the proposal of the parliamentary leader of the CDU in the Bremen state legislature to burn the books of non-conformist authors, such as collections of the poetry of Erich Fried.

guard. In no imperialist country has a severe (let alone decisive) defeat been inflicted on the working class. The rate of surplus-value has not risen in a proportion at all commensurate with the gravity of the capitalist crisis and the historic designs of capital.

Nonetheless, the working class and the workers' movement have remained generally on the defensive up to now. Nowhere have they been able to use the extremely serious crisis of capitalism to challenge the system fundamentally (except in Portugal in 1975). Even in Spain, where the scope of combativity and politicization has been greatest, the conquest of democratic rights and the fall of the dictatorship under the hammer blows of the masses have not (yet) been transformed into a generalized offensive against the capitalist system itself.

Granted, the possibility of such revolutionary crises remains real in the four countries of southwest Europe. It could even spread to a number of countries situated further north. For the moment, however, this has not happened. The reason is clear: even though the objective strength and degree of organization of the working class are higher than ever, and even though a new workers' vanguard contesting the hegemony of the old bureaucratic apparatuses has indeed emerged in many factories and unions throughout capitalist Europe (less so in Japan and North America, but these countries will follow the same road, with several years' delay), the curbing and disorienting role of the traditional bureaucratic apparatuses remains enormous, in the absence of a political force in the workers' movement strong enough to counter them credibly.

The mass organizations of the European workers' movement were living in the euphoria of 'permanent' growth guaranteeing full employment and social progress. The traumatic shock of four years of massive – and rising! – unemployment has brought them down to earth. But the bourgeoisie launched a colossal campaign of mystification among the working class to 'explain' that the crisis was the result of shortages and not of overproduction. The aim of this campaign is to blame the crisis on the colonial peoples and the western trade unions and toiling masses, claiming that they are responsible for massive unemployment. The theoretical and political disarray of the leaderships of the unions and the mass workers' parties in the West in face of this ideological offensive of the bourgeoisie has been complete. Nearly all have made concession after concession, some yielding on each and every point.

Now, although the sixties and the beginning of the seventies saw the emergence of a whole generation of vanguard union militants in the factories who were perfectly capable of reacting against attacks on purchasing power under conditions of full employment – independently of the bureaucratic apparatuses and even in opposition to them if need be – this vanguard still lacks experience in how to respond to factory closures and layoffs during a period of massive unemployment. Moreover, these vanguard militants have a confused understanding of the fact that such fragmentary reactions are of very limited effectiveness and that comprehensive political responses to the crisis are indispensable. Such comprehensive political responses, however, have not been forthcoming under the conditions of theoretical and programmatic disarray in which the 'official' left is mired. (The small size of the revolutionary organizations, which have not yet crossed the threshold of immediate political credibility in the eyes of the masses, is also a factor here.)

This disarray has been further aggravated by the new popularity of neo-Ricardian conceptions (of the Cambridge school) among economists integrated into the workers' movement, including the Communist Parties (particularly the Italian Communist Party). For the neo-Ricardians, the rate of profit is a simple function of the level of wages. The organic composition of capital is of no concern. They therefore claim that the rise in wages accounts for the fall in profits. It is only a small step from that notion to the conclusion, upheld by the employers, that 'excessive' wage demands eliminate jobs and are responsible for unemployment.[19] Not a few economists associated with the workers' movement, including many

---

[19] See, among many employers' representatives, Professor Wolfram Engels of Germany: '. . . over the years, real wages have risen faster than productivity, and that produces unemployment' (*Wirtschaftswoche*, 23 December 1977).

Social Democratic leaders, have cheerfully taken that step.

It thus becomes clear that *apparently academic theoretical debates are now acquiring an immediate social, political, and practical function in the class struggle.* Only the Marxist explanation for the fall in the rate of profit – as a function of the rising organic composition of capital and not rising wages – can solidly ground the resistance of the unions and the workers to the guilt-projecting ideological offensive of the bourgeoisie, which has a manifestly practical aim: to make the unions accept reductions in real wages and an 'incomes policy' that deprives them of the right to defend the interests of their members, including their unrestricted right to strike.[20]

The right-wing Social Democrats have long since broken with Marxism and peddled the classic banalities of bourgeois ideology within the working class: 'We are all in the same boat. We must all defend the company' (or the national economy, or Europe, or the 'free world', depending on the circumstances). In a number of European countries it is the Social Democratic leaders who have become the major advocates and practitioners of the austerity policy demanded by the bourgeoisie, particularly in Britain, West Germany, Portugal, and Denmark. Some 'Eurocommunist' parties have trailed resolutely in their wake, sometimes even overtaking them in the 'boldness' of the commitment to austerity.[21] This is particularly true of the Italian and Spanish Communist parties. The Portuguese Communist Party has adopted a more mitigated position, covering for the

[20] For years John Kenneth Galbraith has been calling for a compulsory incomes policy, i.e. a severe restriction (if not elimination) of the freedom to negotiate wages and the right to strike. His aim is to escape from the dilemma: massive unemployment or accelerated inflation. These positions are systematically defended in his latest work, *Money*, Harmondsworth, 1976, pp. 289–95; 321–26. Most more or less moderate American Keynesians have been faithfully dogging his steps.

[21] See especially Enrico Berlinguer, *Austerità, occasione per trasformare l'Italia*, Editori Riuniti, Rome, 1977. In a sensational interview accorded the newspaper *Repubblica* in early 1978 Lucio Lama, the Communist trade-union leader, went even further in this direction. See also the article by Miguel Boyer, the major economist of the Spanish Socialist Workers Party (PSOE), in *El Socialista*, 6 November 1977, which asserts that any attempt by the workers to augment their share of a declining national income would automatically raise unemployment.

austerity policy in principle and in deeds but opposing certain specific austerity measures under the pressure of its working-class base.

The French Communist Party is the only mass workers' party in Europe that has pronounced itself, for the moment, resolutely against any austerity policy, in the name of a classical Keynesian anti-crisis orientation. Most of the left Social Democratic currents share this position (the Labour Left in Britain, the CERES in France, Fraternidade Operaria in Portugal, the Renardist trade-union left in Belgium, etc.). Up to now, however, none of these currents has lastingly resisted approval of austerity measures in deeds the moment they shift from opposition to participation in cabinets. It is not likely that the French Communist Party would act differently.

The arguments with which the right-wing Social Democrats and Eurocommunists justify their option for austerity policies are of two varieties. The first is essentially political. It boils down to the everlasting refrain of 'lesser evilism': 'If we don't manage the crisis reaction will, and then austerity will be much more severe. Moreover, if we do not allow capitalism to extract itself from the crisis through austerity, unemployment will provoke a return of the far right to power, even absolute catastrophe.' In other words: 'Let them cut three fingers off, otherwise you'll lose the whole hand.'

This defeatist argument is not supported by a shred of serious demonstration. Who has proven that the workers would be unable to oppose a wage freeze or a reduction in real wages if they organized an energetic and united struggle? Who has demonstrated that rightist governments would automatically succeed in breaking the resistance of the workers? Have they forgotten the heavy defeat the British miners inflicted on the anti-union offensive of the Heath government? Who has proven that the re-emergence of fascist gangs implies their inevitable victory? Have they forgotten what happened in July 1936 in the proletarian centres in Spain and what happened in Italy during the sixties?

The second argument is of a more strictly economic character, even apparently technical. The right wing of the workers' movement claims that unless consumer spending is reduced (which means, essentially, cutting the wage bill), no growth in investment and therefore no re-establishment of full employment will be possible. To put it in the demagogic words of Helmut Schmidt: 'Today's profits are tomorrow's jobs.'

As it happens, even from the purely technical point of view – that is, if we place ourselves strictly in the framework of the capitalist mode of production – the argument is fallacious. It is based on the simplistic and erroneous hypothesis[22] that the resources of each nation are divided into two great funds: household consumer funds (essentially wages) and productive investment funds. In reality this is not the case at all. Not two but three great categories of spending must be distinguished: the consumption funds of the productive class (in which we include social security payments, i.e. the incomes of all members of the proletariat who are not in a position to sell their labour-power for whatever reason: retirement, illness, injury, unemployment, pregnancy, professional training or re-training, etc.); the productive investment fund; and the unproductive investment fund. The latter category includes not only the expenditures of public administration, military spending, and the costs of maintaining the ruling class and its agents and servants, but also those distribution and sales costs caused by the anarchy of the capitalist system, hoarded savings, savings used for speculative purposes, capital shipped out of the country clandestinely, and so on.

It is thus apparent that it is perfectly possible for the first fund to be reduced through austerity measures without any resulting growth in the second fund. In that event, the 'forced savings' of the wage earners simply fuel unproductive spending. It is even possible for the second fund to shrink along with the first. This is precisely what happened in 1975, and it now seems to be happening again in many imperialist countries.

The identification of productive investment and the creation of new jobs is another delusion. Indeed, a growing mass of

[22] There is a striking parallel with the Stalinist axiom that absolute priority must be accorded heavy industry in the process of 'building socialism'. This axiom is grounded theoretically on the same rigidly bi-sectoral hypothesis.

investment is directed towards rationalization, which *elimin-ates* more jobs in the industries to which it is applied than it creates in the branches furnishing equipment goods.

As massive unemployment becomes chronic and worsens, this crudest form of the argument for austerity loses its credibility among the organized workers. Their irritation, even indignation, at the inability of governments, whether 'left' or 'right', to re-establish full employment mounts constantly.

The advocates of class collaboration and the partisans of the rise of capitalist profits are then compelled to withdraw to new defence lines. 'Economic rectification', they say, would be possible only through a vigorous expansion of exports and a serious contraction of imports.[23] Now, the competitive position of national industry on the world market allegedly depends on the 'moderation' of wage increases. Thus, austerity is needed to assure 'recovery through exports'.

Here again, the thesis is contradicted by empirical facts. Table 53 clearly demonstrates that there is no correlation

Table 53
Rate of Increase of Real Wages and Rate of Increase of Exports
(all figures in %)

	A Overall real gains 1976	B Real hourly wages 1976	1977	C Exports (in volume) 1976	1977
United States	+2.2	+2.6	+2.25	+ 3.5	+ 1.75
Britain	−2.4	+1.2	−3.75	+ 7.4	+10.6
France	+4.7	+3.0	+3.1	+ 8.5	+ 6.25
West Germany	+2.6	+2.0	+4.0	+12.4	+ 5.0
Japan	+0.7	+4.3	+2.75	+21.8	+ 5.5
Italy	+5.7	+4.4	+7.75	+11.7	+ 7.0

Sources: For column *A*: Bank for International Settlements, *47e Rapport Annuel*, op. cit., p. 46. For columns *B* and *C*: *Perspectives économiques de l'OCDE*, no. 22, December 1977.

[23] See both the Socialist Party: *89 Réponses aux questions économiques* (Paris, 1977, pp. 107–8) and the economists of the French Communist Party Boccara, Herzog, Le Pors, and Quin: *Changer l'Economie* (Paris, 1977, pp. 90–91, 97, and 149–50).

between moderate rates of wage increases and successful export offensives. This lack of correlation is especially striking if one compares Britain and Italy on the one hand with the United States, Japan, and West Germany on the other. Industrial competitive strength depends essentially on unit costs. And these are determined much more by such factors as technological advances, sequential savings, relative abundance of capital, correct specialization choices, the cost of credit, access to cheaper energy sources and raw materials, and the weight of indebtedness, than by marginal fluctuations in the rate of wage increases. Moreover, it should not be forgotten that wage costs represent only 25–30% of production costs in manufacturing industry, sometimes even less.

In addition, it is strikingly evident that any idea that there can be an 'economic upturn through export growth' in all the imperialist countries at the same time is completely unrealistic. At a time when the world market is expanding only slightly, or even contracting, gains in one quarter must be losses in another. Thus, if the reformist unions and workers' parties associate themselves with the export offensive of their own employers, they do so not only at the expense of the wages of the workers in their own country but also at the expense of the jobs of their class brothers and sisters in other countries. The support the American trade-union bureaucracy has accorded both protectionism and the 'expulsion of illegal immigrants' is but an extreme example of a much more general trend. These hacks of corporatist unionism have replaced the proud slogan 'Workers of all countries unite!' with a lovely new watchword: 'Workers of all countries, eliminate one another's jobs and condemn one another to unemployment and wage cuts!'[24]

The employers in each country constantly invoke the imperatives of international competition to justify their opposi-

[24] Willem de Brees sr., Social Democratic former Dutch prime minister, affirmed in an interview with the *Bulletin économique* of the Free University of Amsterdam (May 1977): 'The mass of unemployment is caused by the fact that we in the Netherlands have foreign workers doing jobs that could be done by Dutch. . . . We should have gradually sent these foreign workers home as more and more Dutch workers became available. . . . But in any event, we must strictly eliminate the (foreign) workers who are here without permission.'

tion to the only measure that could really reabsorb unemployment rapidly: a substantial reduction in the workweek with no reduction in weekly pay and without modification of the organization of labour; in other words, the compulsory employment of additional workers. A large number of trade-union organizations in Western Europe have called for the introduction of the thirty-six (or thirty-five) hour week. There must be an immediate campaign of struggle throughout Europe – if possible even including North America and Japan – for the 35–36 hour week, leading to a European-wide general strike in support of this objective.

But how can one credibly struggle for the 35–36 hour week *throughout Europe* while simultaneously joining the struggle of 'one's own' employer to stimulate 'his' exports and strengthen 'his' competitive position (at the expense of the position of his neighbour)?[25] Participate in international capitalist competition or practise international workers' solidarity – these are two, mutually exclusive lines of action.

Those who reject austerity generally opt instead for Keynesian pump-priming techniques. They claim that to increase the purchasing power of the workers, especially the poorest layers of the population (people who immediately spend their additional incomes), is to create additional markets for consumer goods, which would set economic growth back on the rails (albeit growth of a type different from that of the fifties and sixties, with greater social consumption). The Common Programme in France has pointed this direction; the French Communist Party in particular insists on it.[26]

It is incontestable that an increase in the incomes of the poorer sectors can act as an immediate 'multiplier' and can rapidly turn into a serious upturn in the consumer goods

[25] At its fourth congress (autumn 1977) the PSUC (Catalan section of the Communist Party of Spain) adopted a document on economic policy explicitly axed around the struggle against inflation and for the 'reestablishment of the competitive strength and profitability of companies'.

[26] This neo-Keynesian orientation of the French Communist Party is in clear contradiction with the theory that the crisis is caused by the fall in the rate of profit, upheld in particular by Paul Boccara, the PCF's major economist, in a collectively written work entitled *La Crise*, Paris, 1975, p. 53.

sector, especially if significant unused production capacity exists in this sector. All the experience of the past forty-five years attests to this.

This experience also confirms, however, that there is no automatic transformation of this upturn into a large-scale upswing in productive investment and a complete reabsorption of unemployment (note that even the Rooseveltian New Deal failed in this regard). Experience shows that it is impossible to prevent vigorous reactions from the bourgeoisie the moment the rise in real incomes of the workers exceeds the threshold at which the division of the national income between wages and total surplus-value is seriously altered. These reactions take various forms: capital flight, investment strike, economic sabotage, financial conspiracies (as well as politico-military-terrorist conspiracies) against the 'left' government, etc.

So long as the capitalist mode of production is maintained and the country in question remains integrated into the international capitalist economy, these two factors lead inevitably to accelerated and even galloping inflation, the 'natural mechanism' by which the capitalist system takes from the workers what they had previously won.

Some people, among them Stuart Holland, theoretician of the British Labour Left, have denied that Keynesian pump-priming techniques necessarily have inflationary effects.[27] They see inflation as merely the combined result of the recovery and the fiscal crisis of the state, caused by the bourgeoisie's refusal to 'pay enough taxes'. But is there any way to alter this behaviour of the bourgeoisie, which conforms to the logic of the accumulation of capital, apart from the expropriation of the bourgeoisie?

Hence, recourse to Keynesian priming techniques can have only very limited positive effects, especially limited in time. After a year or two, tensions rise considerably at all levels of social, economic, and political life. *The mixed economy is a myth.* The capitalist economy can be primed and can prosper only in conformity with the logic of capital, i.e. production for

[27] Stuart Holland, *The Socialist Challenge*, London, 1975.

profit. Of course, one can escape these tensions while accepting this logic; but that implies precisely austerity. The only other way to escape them is to expropriate the bourgeoisie and initiate a new and different logic, that of an economy based on the satisfaction of needs, i.e. the logic of the construction of socialism. But to stand midway between the two solutions, to seek to combine them into an alchemistic alloy, is to plunge rapidly into total disorganization of the economy, as in Chile in 1973; in other words, it is to court catastrophe.

The more sophisticated left Social Democrats and left Eurocommunists sometimes strive to take account of the negative balance-sheet of past experiences in Keynesian pump-priming. They thus associate the policy of pump-priming through consumption with a policy of investment control and expansion of the public sector, which is intended to assure the re-establishment of full employment.[28] All the contradictions of the concept of the 'mixed economy' leap to the surface in these proposals.

How can it be assured that investment in the public sector will not compete with growth in the private sector? Who will compel the masters of the trusts to bow to government investment decisions that run counter to their own interests, i.e. which do not simply complement their own plans? How can they be prevented from 'destabilizing' the national economy with the aid of their foreign class brothers, so long as the imperatives of the 'open economy' are accepted? How can all

---

[28] The extension of the public sector is particularly demanded by the PCF, the British Labour Left, and (to a much more moderate degree) the French Socialist Party. The idea of public control of investment has been taken up especially by the British Labour Left and the German Social Democratic Left. For Britain see 'Priority Full Employment', in *The Spokesman*, no. 34 (winter 1977–1978), with contributions in this regard from Stuart Holland, John Hughes, and Ken Coates. For West Germany see *Die Wirtschaftskrise in der BRD*, Baisch, et al. In West Germany a group of economists standing somewhere between the left Social Democracy and the Communist Party, working under the direction of Professor J. Huffschmid, is oriented almost exclusively towards neo-Keynesian solutions through the priming of consumption. During a press conference held in Bonn on 1 May 1977, they demanded an extraordinary budget increase of 20 thousand million DM (nearly $10 thousand million) instead of the paltry 3 thousand million DM decided at the time by the Helmut Schmidt cabinet.

the negative reactions of the bourgeoisie listed above be prevented if the *profitable* monopolies are actually nationalized (the socialization of losses through the nationalization of companies that are losing money obviously serves the interests of big capital)? How can bitter competition between the public and private sectors be prevented from provoking vigorous ripostes from private capital, especially if the public sector spreads to manufacturing industry? How can each expansion of public investment be prevented from being matched by a reduction in private investment, or even a massive capital flight, thus rendering unrealistic the grandiose plans for economic growth (such as the 6% average annual growth rate promised by the leaders of the French Communist Party)?

Under conditions such as these, the class struggle also spreads into the domain of financing. How can the bourgeoisie be compelled to pay the large additional tax burden needed to finance the expansion of the public sector? If the bourgeoisie does not pay, would not the only alternative be austerity for the workers or galloping inflation (which ultimately amounts to the same thing)? Where will the additional resources needed to stimulate mass consumption, social services, and greater public investment come from if the bourgeoisie, acting in its own class interests, refuses to pay? Does not this rapidly lead to a test of strength? In economic terms a test of strength means just this: either expropriate capital or yield to it. In political terms it means: either the conquest of power by the working class or a forcible return to the rule of the bourgeoisie (possibly in its most reactionary form).

Moreover, the advocates of these 'left' solutions weaken their own case by not also demanding a break with the international capitalist market.[29] Hence, their only remaining way out is a combination of increased protectionism – bothersome and ineffective, since it provokes inevitable reactions in the context of the international market – and attempts to cajole the 'national' and international bourgeoisie. The French Socialist Party expresses this contradiction in an especially striking

[29] Cf. Jacques Attali, 'L'acceptation des règles de l'économie mondiale est irréversible' (*La Parole et L'Outil*, Paris).

manner when it asserts: 'Most assuredly, the most powerful and healthiest means by which to check the flight of capital is to set economic development back on the correct path, for economic well-being is the best guarantee of monetary stability. Now, today only the Left is capable of successfully effecting this economic rectification'. Is there any such thing as 'economic well-being' independent of class interest? Will the bourgeoisie warmly applaud an increase in production if it is accompanied by a hard-hitting tax on capital? Will it allow itself to be seduced by a massive increase in the volume of production of ski boots and Citroën *deux-chevaux* even if some of its best factories are expropriated and its total profits are cut in half? Is the bourgeoisie's 'holiest of holies' the index of industrial production, real wages, and employment? Isn't it rather the mass and rate of profit? Do the economists of the French Socialist Party really believe that they can implement the Common Programme while still increasing the mass and rate of private profit? And if this is not the case, won't the bourgeoisie – national and international – consider the economic situation 'unhealthy' and won't it then begin the flight of capital, regardless of the index of industrial production? Once again, the concept of the 'mixed economy' proves to be a dangerous and disorienting myth. It threatens to become a real trap for the working class and the workers' movement.

The crisis and the re-emergence of massive unemployment are organic products of the capitalist system. They cannot be overcome within the framework of the system except by a sharp deterioration in the living and working conditions of the workers. To reject this deterioration is possible only by rejecting the capitalist system and initiating the construction of a qualitatively different economic system.

To be sure, the workers' movement cannot be content to fight the crisis with the mere proclamation of the need for a general anti-capitalist struggle; to do so would entail division, demoralization, and certain defeat. The crisis confronts the workers with alarming concrete problems: layoffs, job losses, factory closures, attacks on wages and social security, speed-up, attacks on previously acquired trade-union and political rights. To reject the defensive fight for immediate demands under the pretext that 'there is no way out within the framework of capitalism' is to condemn oneself and the entire working class to impotence.

In any event, the working class will not follow dogmatists who mount that particular hobby-horse. The workers have already shown that they are prepared to fight stubbornly to defend every gain, every threatened job. The elementary duty of revolutionary Marxists is to support this struggle with all their might, proposing the most effective demands and organizational forms. The 35–36 hour week, a sliding scale of wages (its defence or conquest, depending on the conditions in each country), the defence of the right to strike and the freedom to negotiate wages, the struggle for solidarity with the hardest hit sectors – immigrant workers, women, youth, old people, the unemployed; such are the prime imperatives of this essentially defensive struggle.

To the argument of the employers and reformists that these demands undermine company profits and threaten to exacerbate the crisis the reply is that, given the choice between defence of the physical and moral integrity of our class and defence of capital's profits, we opt resolutely to defend our class, against the defence of profit. If full employment and a decent standard of living have become incompatible with capitalism, the employers have only to depart.

There will be some reformists (and ultra-leftists too) who respond that the logic of capitalism cannot be overturned factory by factory, industry by industry, region by region, or even country by country, but only as a whole; while awaiting the general combat against international capitalism (simultaneously in all countries, of course), a combat that will assuredly consign this system to the dustbin of history, they say, one must yield to this logic of capital. The answer to this argument is simple: everything has a beginning. It is perfectly possible to defeat an employer or a sector of the employers if the working class is united, resolute, and develops a leadership that is up to the task. There is no better way to unleash a general combat than to wage some partial battles that achieve complete success and thus show the workers in practice that it is possible to defend existing employment, wages, and rights.

It is true, however, that any success in the defensive struggle remains only *fragmentary and provisional*. In the long run the logic of capital will reassert itself so long as we remain under the capitalist system. This logic of capital particularly works against the working class during a period of massive unemployment and economic depression. That is why any defensive combat must be integrated into an overall anti-capitalist strategy that seeks to foster, by all possible means, a mobilization of the working class around transitional demands directed against the fundamental causes of the evils from which the workers suffer. During a phase of economic depression, such transitional demands should include, in particular: the expropriation of all companies that close down or lay off masses of workers, and their management at state expense and under workers' control; the nationalization without compensation and with no re-sale of all credit institutions, key industries, and monopolies, whether 'national' or multinational, and their management under workers' control; generalized workers' control over hiring and the organization of labour, which implies veto power over any layoffs; the elaboration by the workers' and people's organizations, based on a network of democratically elected committees whose members can be recalled at the will of the electors, of a plan of economic rectification and development focussed on the satisfaction of the needs of the masses; the development of public enterprises towards this end and the halt to all subsidies to private companies (or the nationalization of all companies receiving subsidies); formation of a government of the workers' organizations to apply all these measures. The struggle for all these demands should lead to the creation of a vast network of committees in the factories, offices, and neighbourhoods to control the application of the programme and counter the sabotage of the bourgeoisie. This network of committees must also ensure the general arming of the toiling people to counter any 'national' or international militaro-fascist conspiracies and should establish fraternal relations of collaboration on an equal basis with the peoples of the 'third world' and with the workers and workers' organizations throughout the world, especially those of Europe.

This transitional programme would open the road to the construction of a democratic, self-managed, and planned socialist society based on the power of workers' councils – with a non-exclusive multiparty system and the maintenance, consolidation, and extension of all political freedoms for all citizens. To fight for such an alternative to capitalism, now caught in an impasse, is to oppose the prospect of unemployment, austerity, and growing repression with the only real and effective alternative worthy of the efforts of the toiling masses.

31 January 1978

Index